GameSkills

A Fun Approach to Learning Sport Skills

GameSkills

A Fun Approach to Learning Sport Skills

Stephanie J. Hanrahan, PhD
Teresa B. Carlson, EdD

The University of Queensland

Human Kinetics

Library of Congress Cataloging-in-Publication Data

Hanrahan, Stephanie J., 1961-
  Game skills : a fun approach to learning sport skills / Stephanie J. Hanrahan,
Teresa B. Carlson.
      p. cm.
  ISBN 0-7360-0203-0
  1. Physical education and training–Curricula. I. Carlson, Teresa B., 1955- II.
Title.

GV363 .H28 2000
796'.07'7–dc21   99-057711

ISBN: 0-7360-0203-0

Acquisitions Editor: Scott Wikgren; **Developmental Editor:** Lynn M. Hooper-
Davenport; **Assistant Editors:** Amanda S. Ewing, Mark Zulauf; **Copyeditor:** Bar-
bara Walsh; **Proofreader:** Laura Ward Majersky; **Graphic Designer:** Robert
Reuther; **Graphic Artist:** Kim Maxey; **Cover Designer:** Jack W. Davis; **Photogra-
pher (cover):** Tom Roberts; **Art Manager:** Craig Newsom; **Illustrators:** Deborah
Noon (diagram art) and Tim Shedelbower (figure drawings); **Printer:** Versa Press.

Printed in the United States of America   10 9 8 7 6 5 4 3 2 1

Human Kinetics
Web site: http://www.humankinetics.com/

United States: Human Kinetics
P.O. Box 5076
Champaign, IL 61825-5076
1-800-747-4457
e-mail: humank@hkusa.com

Canada: Human Kinetics
475 Devonshire Road Unit 100
Windsor, ON N8Y 2L5
1-800-465-7301 (in Canada only)
e-mail: humank@hkcanada.com

Europe: Human Kinetics, P.O. Box IW14
Leeds LS16 6TR, United Kingdom
+44 (0)113-278 1708
e-mail: humank@hkeurope.com

Australia: Human Kinetics
57A Price Avenue
Lower Mitcham, South Australia 5062
(08) 82771555
e-mail: liahka@senet.com.au

New Zealand: Human Kinetics
P.O. Box 105-231, Auckland Central
09-523-3462
e-mail: humank@hknewz.com

Contents

Key to Icons

Agility
(working on nimbleness or dexterity)

Balance
(without balance individuals cannot control voluntary movement)

Cardiovascular Endurance
(getting the heart rate up and keeping it up)

Concentration and Attention
(learning to pay attention to what's important and ignore what's not)

Coordination
(working on fluidity of movement and timing)

Flexibility
(increasing range of motion)

Getting to Know Each Other
(learning names)

Integrated Games
(integrating individuals with disabilities)

Organization and Transitions
(dividing into groups or moving from one activity to another)

Power and Speed
(making quick and powerful movements)

Strength
(lifting, pushing, or pulling against a large force)

Tactics and Strategies
(devising or employing plans of action)

Team Building
(working effectively in groups)

Activity Finder

ACTIVITY	AGES												
1.1 Birthday Brigades	8+								◆	◆			
1.2 Color Categories	8+								◆	◆			
1.3 Size Systems	8+									◆			
1.4 Random Draw	8+								◆	◆			
1.5 Undies Unite	18+									◆			
1.6 Distance Counts	13+								◆	◆			
1.7 Loopy Labels	8+							◆		◆			
1.8 Halving by Habits	8+							◆	◆	◆			
1.9 Squatting Squads	8+									◆			
2.1 Fortune Cookies	13+	◆		◆			◆	◆	◆	◆		◆	
2.2 Touch 'n' Go	8+									◆			
2.3 High Five	8+	◆		◆				◆	◆	◆			
2.4 Roll 'n' Go	8+	◆		◆			◆		◆	◆	◆	◆	◆

(continued)

Activity Finder

ACTIVITY	AGES															
3.15 Nose and Toes	8+	◆		◆					◆							
3.16 It's in the Middle	8+				◆						◆					
3.17 Obstacle Tag	8+	◆				◆										
4.1 Passing Tag	13+	◆			◆	◆	◆									◆
4.2 Help Me Tag	8+					◆			◆							
4.3 Thieves	13+	◆			◆	◆			◆							
4.4 Protect Your Turf	13+				◆	◆			◆						◆	
4.5 Ball Pair Tag	8+	◆				◆	◆		◆							
5.1 Lofty Leaps	8+							◆		◆				◆		
5.2 Dare to Be Dizzy	13+	◆	◆							◆			◆			
5.3 Rock and Roll	18+		◆			◆			◆					◆	◆	
5.4 Roll Up	8+			◆						◆						
5.5 No Elephants Allowed	8+		◆						◆				◆			

Activity	Age	C1	C2	C3	C4	C5	C6	C7	C8	C9	C10	C11	C12
5.6 Circle Walk	13+			◆		◆							
6.1 Have You Ever...?	8+						◆						
6.2 Pretzels	8+	◆				◆	◆	◆					
6.3 Find It Fast	8+	◆					◆				◆		
6.4 See No Obstacles	13+	◆	◆										
6.5 Blindfold Run	18+	◆								◆		◆	
6.6 The Barricade	13+	◆			◆				◆	◆			
6.7 Pendulum	13+	◆								◆			
6.8 Blowing in the Breeze	13+	◆								◆			
6.9 Catch Me!	18+	◆		◆						◆			
6.10 Minefield	13+	◆	◆							◆		◆	
6.11 Group Push-Up	18+	◆	◆	◆									
6.12 Use It or Lose It	13+	◆				◆							
7.1 Toe Tapper	8+		◆							◆			◆
7.2 Knee Tag	8+		◆							◆			◆

(continued)

Activity Finder

ACTIVITY	AGES	1	2	3	4	5	6	7	8	9	10	11	12	13
7.3 Sock Stealing	18+	◆						◆					◆	
7.4 Tug-to-Win	8+						◆		◆		◆	◆		
7.5 Leg Wrestling	8+						◆		◆			◆		
7.6 Thumb Wrestling	8+				◆	◆					◆	◆		
7.7 Lock 'n' Pull	8+						◆				◆	◆		
7.8 Fake and Push	8+						◆				◆	◆	◆	
7.9 Blow It	8+												◆	
8.1 Pair Pull-Ups	13+							◆						
8.2 Keep It Up	8+			◆		◆					◆	◆		
8.3 Push to Stand	8+						◆					◆		
8.4 Fantasy Writing	8+						◆			◆	◆	◆		
8.5 Dry Surfing	8+						◆				◆	◆		
8.6 Imaginary Skipping	8+			◆		◆		◆						

Activity	Age
8.7 Basket Case	8+
9.1 Tunnel Ball Plus	13+
9.2 Over-Under	8+
9.3 Dizzy Relay	13+
9.4 Team Jump	8+
9.5 Progressive Relay	8+
9.6 Collective Tally	8+
9.7 Missing Something	8+
9.8 Leading Lines	8+
9.9 Obstacle Options	8+
10.1 Beat the Ball	8+
10.2 Shadow	8+
10.3 Striptease	13+
10.4 Keep It Rolling	8+
10.5 Do It in the Dark	8+

xiii

Activity Finder

ACTIVITY	AGES													
10.6 Swap It	8+								♦					
11.1 Touch It	8+	♦	♦							♦				
11.2 Charge!	8+		♦		♦				♦					
11.3 Bucket Brigade	8+		♦		♦				♦					
11.4 David and Goliath	13+		♦		♦		♦		♦					
11.5 Experience It All	8+	♦			♦				♦					
11.6 Add-a-Ball	8+							♦	♦	♦	♦			
11.7 Continuous Challenge	13+				♦			♦	♦	♦				
12.1 Pseudo Soccer	8+		♦	♦					♦		♦	♦		
12.2 Pick a Hand	13+				♦			♦						
12.3 Get It First	8+		♦		♦					♦	♦			
12.4 Keep Away Kapers	8+		♦								♦			
12.5 Stop and Hoard	8+		♦					♦	♦	♦	♦			

Preface

Have you ever been halfway through a semester of teaching or a season of coaching and sighed to yourself, "Aarrghh, 10 more weeks to go!" Your enthusiasm has waned, and your students or athletes look like they'd rather be anywhere else. They may perk up for games or competition, but skills practice has become a drag—something they endure rather than enjoy. Teachers and coaches as well as students and athletes can get stuck in a stale, predictable groove.

Wouldn't it be great to work with enthusiastic, motivated students or athletes, with the entire class or team (teachers and coaches, too) actually looking forward to every session? By incorporating the activities in this book into your sessions, you can resurrect (or initially create) the spark that will lift the class's or team's level of effort, enjoyment, and achievement. Whether you want a fun, fast, and furious start to a session; a team-building game; an activity to increase strength, flexibility, or cardiovascular endurance; or a challenge to help individuals develop tactics, strategies, or concentration skills, you will find what you need in this book.

Chapters 1 to 10 contain games that are appropriate for individuals participating in almost any sport, with almost a quarter of them suitable for use in the pool as well as on dry land. Chapter 11 focuses on the fielding and striking sports of baseball, cricket, and softball, yet contains two games appropriate for other sports. The games in chapter 12 are designed for invasion sports such as soccer, basketball, and hockey—sports that require one team to invade the territory of another team to score. Again, two of the games in chapter 12 are appropriate for other sports. Chapter 13 covers exclusively the net games of volleyball, tennis, badminton, and table tennis. All of the activities in chapter 14 take place in the water. However, swimmers and other water sports participants will benefit from doing many of the activities in other chapters, and similarly, participants in land-based sports will benefit from some water sessions.

The authors of this book have been on both sides of the fence—as students and athletes and as physical education teachers and coaches. Stephanie has been an international-level volleyball player and a professional ice skater as well as a swim and skating instructor and a volleyball coach. In addition, she has worked with teachers and coaches for more than 10 years as a sport psychologist. Teresa has competed in swimming for more than 20 years and has worked as a physical education teacher in Botswana, Australia, Pakistan, and the United States. Her involvement in schools has included coaching netball, basketball, and track and field. Both authors have extensive experience in coach and teacher education. At times, we have been bored, frustrated, and lethargic as both participants and leaders. Instead of getting sucked into doing the same old thing every day, we have learned, as have many of you, that incorporating fun and challenge into all levels of physical activity involvement reaps many rewards. We have acquired our repertoire of activities over many years, and our sport science training has allowed us to delete those activities likely to injure participants.

Even the most exciting game or activity can become boring if used repeatedly. Needless repetition should no longer be an issue, as this book provides a resource of more than 100 activities coded for easy selection on the basis of your needs. The Activity Finder at the front of the book indicates the benefit(s) of each activity, as well as the age range that is most appropriate. For example, if fitness instructors want to find activities to develop flexibility, if coaches require tasks to enhance concentration, or if teachers want to focus on speed, it will be easy for them to scan the appropriate column to determine the suitable activities. The benefits (in alphabetical order) included in the Activity Finder are as follows:

Agility—develops nimbleness or dexterity

Balance—without balance, individuals cannot control voluntary movement

Cardiovascular endurance—gets the heart rate up and keeps it up

Concentration and attention—teaches participants to pay attention to what's important and ignore what's not

Coordination—develops fluidity of movement and timing

Flexibility—increases range of motion

Getting to know each other—helps participants learn each other's names

Integrated games—integrates individuals with disabilities

Organization and transitions—divides participants into groups or moves them from one activity to another

Power and speed—participants make quick and powerful movements

Strength—participants lift, push, or pull against a large force

Tactics and strategies—participants must devise or employ plans of action

Team building—participants must devise or employ plans of action

Many books available in the marketplace contain activities and games for children. All the games described in this book have been successfully tried out on high school–aged students and adults, although most of them can still be used with children. The majority of the activities are appropriate for participants age 8 and older. Approximately 20% of the games target those who are 13 or older, and about 5% target adults only.

Fun is an essential requirement for an activity's inclusion in this book. However, each game or activity brings additional benefits. The standard structure for each activity is as follows:

Activity Name

Age Range

Benefits

The Basics (how to play the game)

How Many Participants?

What Type of Equipment?

Where?

Safety Considerations

Helpful Hints

Extensions and Variations

Although this book is written primarily for physical education teachers and coaches, individuals involved in leading physical activities of any type (e.g., fitness instructors or scout leaders) will find useful games, hints, and ideas.

Keep in mind that we titled the activities in this book to be catchy and fun. The activity names have served this purpose well with those who we've taught and coached. If, however, you feel particular activity names aren't appropriate for those who you teach or coach, you can certainly change the titles when you use the activities with your team or class (e.g., you can refer to ("Do It in the Dark" as "In the Dark"). Remember that fun and enthusiasm—as well as skill building—are the most important elements of the games in this book.

As noted earlier, safety considerations are specified for each activity. Our safety issues not only consider physical safety (avoiding injury), but also emotional safety (avoiding embarrassment). However, all teachers, coaches, and leaders should follow the safety policies of their district, organization, or school, whether the activity is held in a gym or pool or on a rink, field, or court.

Acknowledgments

We would like to thank the students and staff in the Department of Human Movement Studies at The University of Queensland who voluntarily played all of our games. Our thanks also go to various sports teams that provided willing guinea pigs.

We would like to name the individuals who read, led, and gave us valuable feedback on our games: Joe Baker, Kirsten Blake, Peter Frederiksen, Hamish Millard, and Angela O'Connor. We are also grateful to those individuals who proofread games or allowed themselves to be grabbed in the hallway and coerced into initial trials.

We are deeply indebted to Deb Noon for the computer graphics and to Tim Shedelbower for the line drawings in this book.

Activities for Splitting Into Groups

Standing around waiting for something to happen, continually counting off by numbers, and worrying that you'll be the last player picked for a team are all experiences people like to avoid. Not only are they time-consuming, they can diminish the group's enthusiasm and at times cause cliques to form, making some individuals feel isolated and unwanted.

The activities in this section are designed to enliven the environment, provide smooth transitions, divide people quickly, and make people laugh. They will also help the group leader avoid encountering the rolling eyes and groans of disgust that can accompany traditional group selection. The randomness of the techniques also keeps individuals from feeling as if they have been picked on or forced to work (or play!) with particular individuals. This chapter provides quick, fun, random ways of dividing individuals into groups or teams.

1.1   BIRTHDAY BRIGADES

8+

The Basics
Everyone has a birthday. Using birthdays for group division can result in any number of groups you require—from 2 (half of the year) to 31 (day of the month). People line up in order of their birthdays. Individuals can then be peeled off to form groups of a specified number. No adaptations or alterations are needed to include participants with disabilities in this activity.

How Many Participants?
Ten or more.

What Type of Equipment?
No equipment needed!

Where?
Anywhere!

Safety Considerations
When working with adults (particularly of the more mature vintage), deliberately avoiding any division by year of birth may help prevent embarrassment or lying among participants.

Helpful Hints
Although these transition games are designed to avoid disgruntlement in terms of team or group selection, occasionally you will get a negative verbal or visual response from a participant. How you deal with this will vary based on the age and maturity of the participants, and your [the leader's] experience. Although the best way to handle this reaction will depend on the particular individuals involved, be sure to deal with it immediately. Generally, if you've established ground rules from the start that forbid putting anyone down, including yourself, you can gently remind the participant to stop such behavior at once. A quiet word out of the limelight to the groaner will avoid escalating the situation.

Extensions and Variations
⑥ Signs of the Zodiac or the Chinese calendar years can be used as alternatives to birthdays. Introducing something like the Chinese

calendar can enhance multiculturalism; providing a poster of years and animals helps the process.

⑥ If an attendance or team list exists, it is possible to predetermine groups based on the letters in first names, last names, or both. Divisions can be made on the basis of the first or last letter of a name, the existence of a letter anywhere in a name, the occurrence of double letters in a name, or any other combination you can think of.

⑥ Any version of this activity can be made more challenging (and quieter) by including a "no talking" rule. When using birthdays, you can also add the rules of "no writing" and "no showing ID." These restrictions require participants to develop alternate methods of communication, such as using hand signals.

1.2 COLOR CATEGORIES

8+

The Basics
Rather than focusing on the color of skin, use colors in a variety of ways to highlight similarities rather than differences. Individuals group together on the basis of clothing color. When team or school uniforms mean everyone is wearing the same colors, base color categories on pinnies, shoes, hair scrunchies, or socks. If school pinnies are all the same color, distribute pieces of colored yarn (ideally, tie the yarn around people's wrists).

How Many Participants?
Ten or more.

What Type of Equipment?
Pinnies or yarn (if necessary).

Where?
Anywhere!

Safety Considerations
⑥ Colored bands made of stretchy material are occasionally used in schools as a form of team identification. When bands are used, students tend to wear them around their heads rather than around

their waists or arms as intended. Be aware of the possibility that participants could contract head lice.

⑥ In areas where gang membership is signified by the wearing of certain colors, avoid using clothing as a factor for dividing participants into groups.

Helpful Hints

A range of alternatives exists in terms of how pinnies can be distributed. A system that appears to be random is best. Actual random distribution can be used, or you can orchestrate the allocation of pinnies in a manner that strives for group balance but still appears to be random. For example, as part of a running warm-up, the leader can hand out pinnies in a manner that guarantees that all of the fastest athletes will not be in the same group or team. If a skills session benefits from grouping people of like ability, then pinnies can be distributed accordingly. At all times, however, it is useful if the leader appears to be casual about who receives what color.

Classmates or teammates can easily include participants who are visually impaired (and cannot determine color) in the appropriate group. Rarely is specific intervention required by the leader (for example, telling people who are visually impaired what color they are wearing, or immediately linking them up with partners with the same color). In most instances participants look out for each other and automatically include those who may need a bit of help. An alternative is to have people call out the color they are wearing, letting visually impaired individuals pick up on the auditory cues.

Extensions and Variations

Hair color or eye color can be used in place of clothing or pinny color. If using this option, take great care that divisions do not become racial. A problem-free alternative is to have individuals pair up with the requirement that partners have different-colored hair or eyes, or, in a larger group, that no more than half the people in the group have the same color hair or eyes.

1.3   SIZE SYSTEMS

8+

The Basics
This activity is ideal when you want to group together people of similar size (e.g., for trust activities or tackling). Individuals are divided on the basis of height. The simplest method is to have everyone line up from tallest to shortest (or "least tall") and then divide into the number of groups required.

How Many Participants?
Ten or more.

What Type of Equipment?
No equipment needed!

Where?
Anywhere (except maybe the deep end of a pool!).

Safety Considerations
Sometimes the shorter (or very tall adolescents) may be sensitive about height. Focusing on hand size may alter the focus (see Extensions and Variations).

Helpful Hints
If diverse groups are desired, then include at least one person from the first third, the middle third, and the final third of the line in each group, or require that there be at least a 2-inch difference between the heights of partners.

Extensions and Variations
⑥ Individuals can also divide themselves on the basis of hand or foot size. If the class or team is made up of both males and females, then be sure to have people compare the actual size of their feet rather than relying on shoe sizes, because men's and women's shoe sizes differ. Additionally, shoe sizes may become problematic if you have individuals from Europe or Asia, where different sizing systems are used.

⑥ The size of one's family can be used—for example, the number of siblings a person has. (Note: Avoid this option in areas where family size is highly determined by religion or culture.)

⑥ If forming teams for a sport where height is an advantage (e.g., basketball or volleyball), once the line has been formed, every other person steps forward. Those who have stepped forward form one team; the remainder forms the other.

1.4   RANDOM DRAW

8+

The Basics

Rather than just appearing random, this activity genuinely is random. One random draw can be used to group people in a variety of teams. Start with a deck of playing cards. Have the same number of cards as participants. Each individual draws a card. Individuals can then be grouped according to suit or number. If only two groups are required, then people can be divided by color of card or by odd and even cards. Specific cards can also be selected to represent particular duties or roles within a team or group, such as team leaders, referees, scorers, goal-keepers, and timers. Anyone who can see can participate in Random Draw.

How Many Participants?

Four or more.

What Type of Equipment?

Playing cards.

Where?

Anywhere!

Safety Considerations

None that we can identify.

Helpful Hints

⑥ Request that participants return all cards before the initial activity. (You may also request that participants refrain from practicing origami!)

⑥ Remember that one draw can be used for multiple combinations. For example, people can form four groups on the basis of suit and then two groups on the basis of color.

⑥ If using a single draw for multiple combinations, stress that individuals must be able to recall the full details of their cards at the end of the day; this should make it easier for them to redivide within the hour.

Extensions and Variations

Mark the area to be used with cones. Under each cone place one or more objects such as colored pieces of carpet, cards, or colored balloons (uninflated). The number of objects under each cone will depend on the number of participants and the number of cones available. A variety of warm-up activities can be used to get each individual to a cone (see chapter 2). Each person then collects an object under that cone and finds the other individuals with identical objects. For example, everyone who finds a piece of green carpet or a green balloon gets together to form a group.

1.5   UNDIES UNITE

18+

The Basics

This activity is actually another variation of Color Categories. Whenever we have used this transition activity, smiles and laughter have resulted. Individuals group together on the basis of the color or pattern of their underwear! There is no need for participants to actually look at their underwear, as most people can remember what they put on that morning.

How Many Participants?

Ten or more.

What Type of Equipment?

Absolutely nothing, except for an enthusiastic teacher or coach.

Where?

Anywhere except for the pool, where underwear is normally not worn.

Safety Considerations

In rare instances embarrassment can become an issue. Make sure that a supportive environment has been established, and that pressure to show underwear to prove group membership is avoided.

Helpful Hints

Splitting a group into those with solid, light-colored undies on one side and those with bright colors, patterns, or flowers on the other usually results in two fairly even groups. You may want to specify a third group— those who cannot remember what kind of underwear they are wearing. Then, if groups are uneven, the two smaller groups can be combined.

Extensions and Variations

⑥ Particularly with males, the age-old debate of boxers versus briefs can be introduced for an interesting variation.

⑥ To keep the mood light, ask for those wearing no underwear to stand in the middle. (Anyone brave enough to admit it can deal with the consequences!)

1.6   DISTANCE COUNTS

13+

The Basics

Individuals make eye contact with a person across the room. The person with whom eye contact is made needs to be at least 10 feet away. Once everyone has established definite eye contact with someone, people move to join their newfound partners. As people often stand near their best friends, this activity requires people to work (or play) with individuals with whom they may not naturally or automatically socialize, thereby avoiding cliques.

How Many Participants?

Ten or more.

What Type of Equipment?

No equipment needed!

Where?

Any defined area.

Safety Considerations

The leader needs to be alert for individuals who may be overlooked when others refuse to make eye contact with them. Refer to Helpful Hints. This activity is not recommended when there are one or two people who are ostracized by the group.

Helpful Hints

⑥ Before having participants move to join their partners, indicate that anyone who ends up without a partner should move to the middle of the room. As individuals come to the middle, the instructor can quickly and unobtrusively partner them. As everyone tends to move toward the middle anyway when joining their partners, instructor intervention is rarely needed.

⑥ When dealing with an odd number of people, you have multiple options: the teacher or coach becomes involved in the activity; one group of three is formed; or the idea of forming pairs is dropped in favor of larger groups for everyone.

Extensions and Variations

For individuals who are visually impaired, partners who sight them may call out their names. When individuals hear their names, they are responsible for making their way to the caller. If the entire group is visually impaired, then choose alternative splitting activities.

1.7   LOOPY LABELS

8+

The Basics

Each individual is given a label. Groups are formed on the basis of similar labels. Labels can differ in terms of shapes, colors, designs, or all three (see figure on next page for an example). The groups can be created on the basis of more than one aspect of a label. Loopy Labels can easily include names, making this an ideal initial activity.

How Many Participants?

Four or more.

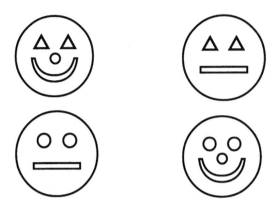

Using these loopy labels, you could have participants form into groups according to eye or mouth shape.

What Type of Equipment?
One label for each person. Labels need to be cut or colored before the session.

Where?
This activity tends to work better indoors.

Safety Considerations
Avoid using any symbols that may be potentially offensive.

Helpful Hints
Be sure that all labels are collected and disposed of properly at the end of the session. This avoids litter, gummy labels in washing machines, and the embarrassment of walking around in public wearing a label.

Extensions and Variations
Participants can create their own labels. You can ask individuals to draw or create symbols of their profession, favorite subject, ideal vacation spot, or favorite dessert. More simply, they can just write their names using one of a variety of colored pens. Groups can then be formed on the basis of color or of other similarities (such as the same favorite subject). This variation encourages creativity and can allow artistic individuals to come to the fore. If participants create their own labels, give them a time limit, because some will tend to create a masterpiece rather than a simple label. If anyone makes a potentially offensive label, quickly provide that individual with a new label and suggest an alternate design.

1.8   HALVING BY HABITS

The Basics

Humans are creatures of habit. Many of us are not aware of the extent of our systematic patterns of behavior. Halving by Habits highlights some of these, encourages the discovery of commonalities, and allows a laugh or two in the process. Individuals are divided on the basis of personal habits. For example, ask participants to cross their arms. Those with the right arm on top form one group; those with the left on top form another. Everyone has habits, including people with disabilities. The habit for the activity can be selected on the basis of the abilities of the people in the group. For example, crossing arms would be appropriate for anyone except for above-elbow arm amputees or individuals who are severely motor impaired. See Extensions and Variations for alternatives.

How Many Participants?

Six or more.

What Type of Equipment?

No equipment needed!

Where?

Anywhere!

Safety Considerations

Should the occasion arise where only one person does the opposite of everyone else, there is the potential for embarrassment. The leader can indicate how special that individual is and then focus attention on a different habit.

Helpful Hints

⑥ If the division results in uneven numbers, the teacher or coach must be prepared to quickly move the required number of people.

⑥ If working with children or adolescents, you can use this activity to spark discussion about how habits are formed and how "different" does not mean "bad."

Extensions and Variations

People can be split into two groups on the basis of a number of habits:

- Each person folds the hands together so the fingers interlock. Which thumb is on top?

- Which side of the bed does each person get out of in the morning?

- Everyone winks. Which eye did each person use?

- Which leg does each person put into her or his pants first?

1.9   SQUATTING SQUADS

8+

The Basics

This is a great activity for moving from pairs to groups. Participants may start a session working (or playing) with a friend or someone of their choice. This activity forces all pairs to split. Within pairs, one person stands and one person squats. All the squatters become one group and all those standing become the other.

How Many Participants?

Six or more.

What Type of Equipment?

No equipment needed!

Where?

Anywhere (although squatters may have trouble breathing in a pool!).

Safety Considerations

For older participants, squatting may be a problem if knees are beginning to show the wear and tear of years of active participation. Heads and tails may be a better alternative (see Helpful Hints).

Helpful Hints

- Inform participants that they are to take their stance (or position) when you yell "Declare!"

- Because Squatting Squads is somewhat basic, leaders need to inject enthusiasm. Demonstrating positions in a rapid or exaggerated manner helps.

Extensions and Variations

◉ Instead of squatting and standing, participants can be asked to form the push-up position or a V-sit (or any other shape or form).

◉ Because most people are familiar with the practice of flipping a coin, participants can be asked to declare whether they are heads or tails (no coins involved). Heads is indicated by placing both hands on one's head, and tails by placing both hands on one's "tail"!

Transition Activities

In both physical education classes and practice sessions for sports, a lot of time can be wasted in trying to move the group from one activity or drill to the next. Transition activities keep participants active while allowing the teacher or coach time to set up the next activity or drill or just take a quick breather. Transition activities are also useful for bringing the group together to receive instructions or allowing the leader to have a quiet word with one participant without the rest of the group listening in. This chapter provides quick, fun ways to move participants from one task to the next.

2.1 FORTUNE COOKIES

13+

The Basics

As you know, a fortune cookie contains a slip of paper with a fortune on it. Rather than doing a lot of baking and intricate inserting of papers, just use the strips of paper by themselves. Each piece of paper describes a group activity or exercise, preferably ones that the group has done before. Each participant is given a fortune at the beginning of the session. When the teacher or coach calls out an individual's name, that person reads out his or her fortune and leads the group in that activity. Unless the fortune states otherwise, the person has 2 minutes to lead the activity listed on the fortune. Fortune Cookies not only provides smooth transitions between activities but also gives all participants an opportunity to experience the leadership role.

How Many Participants?

Four or more.

What Type of Equipment?

"Fortunes"—strips of paper with different activities written on them.

Where?

Anywhere! (If you try this in the pool, you might want to laminate the fortunes.)

Safety Considerations

Although the participants are responsible for leading each activity, the teacher or coach needs to be sure that standard safety procedures are followed at all times. Safety issues may not be obvious to all participants.

Helpful Hints

⑥ The fortune readings can be spread out over an entire session or used rapidly one after the other.

⑥ The focus of the session can be determined by the types of activities included in the fortunes. For example, all activities can focus on developing strength, endurance, flexibility, or agility.

Lead two exercises that develop abdominal strength.

Teach the class how to perform any stretching exercise that requires working with a partner.

Demonstrate an exercise that helps shoulder flexibility.

You have five minutes to increase everyone's heart rate to at least 150 bpm.

Use fortunes like these to keep your group motivated and active as you transition between drills or activities.

◎ If you find a group of activities that works well, you may want to laminate the fortunes rather than rewriting them every time. Fortunes can be color coded to indicate what type of activity they represent.

Extensions and Variations

◎ Have all of the fortunes in one spot. When the teacher or coach calls out a name, that person has to run to the spot, select a fortune, and then quickly lead the activity without any time for preparation.

◎ Have the participants write their own fortunes at the beginning of the session.

◎ For physical education settings, review of theory can be included in this activity by having each leader explain the muscle groups involved in the activity, the biomechanical principles employed, or some other concept that has already been taught.

2.2   TOUCH 'N' GO

8+

The Basics

The teacher or coach calls out, "Everybody touch six different cones and then come in."

Touch 'n' Go is an activity that can last all of 10 seconds. However short, though, it gets people moving and gives the teacher or coach a few vital seconds to collect his or her thoughts about what happens next. This is also a useful activity if you see attention waning and need a quick energizer. Although it is extremely simple, we have included this activity because our experience has demonstrated that teachers and coaches sometimes overlook the obvious.

How Many Participants?

Two or more.

What Type of Equipment?

At least six cones (often these are around anyway, serving as boundary markers or being used in other activities).

Where?

Indoors or outdoors.

Safety Considerations

Heads up! Particularly when people are reaching down to touch a cone or pick up an object, you want to avoid any head butts!

Helpful Hints

If some participants feel that haste or urgency is not required, be prepared to offer a reward of some sort to the people who complete the activity within a specified time. If a single individual appears to lack motivation, ask that person to call out the next transition activity.

Extensions and Variations

⑥ Indoors, touch all four walls (the smart ones learn to go to the corners, where they can touch two walls at once!).

⑥ Touch six intersections of lines (most gyms have lines for multiple sports painted on the floor).

⑥ Collect a specific number of items of equipment and then come in (e.g., collect seven tennis balls on a tennis court).

⑥ As the participants are finishing touching or collecting the required objects, ask everyone to form groups of a specified number. To create a bit of chaos and fun, first request groups of three, then seven, then four, and finally the number of people in each group you actually need for the next activity.

8+

2.3   HIGH FIVE

The Basics
High Five is another quick transition activity, but it encourages individuals to interact with each other. Although simple, this activity is sure to bring smiles to faces. Each individual gives high fives to four different people. A high five involves two people facing each other, jumping straight up off of both feet, and meeting palm to palm in the air with the other person. Include individuals in wheelchairs in this activity by simply deleting the jump requirement.

How Many Participants?
Five or more.

What Type of Equipment?
No equipment needed!

Where?
Anywhere!

Safety Considerations
It may be necessary to remind people that high fives do not require great amounts of force. You may require that all the high fives be done quietly.

Helpful Hints
⑥ To help individuals learn each other's names, have them say their name as they give a high five. After a bit of practice, have them say the name of the other person.

⑥ If some individuals are being excluded, you can require that of the four different people contacted, at least two of them must be blonde, tall, short, or left-handed or must play different positions within the team. The list is endless.

◉ No changes to the activity are needed if it takes place in the shallow end of the pool. The deep-end version of High Five is excellent for water polo practice in that the goal is still to make the high fives as high as possible!

Extensions and Variations

◉ Use high 10s. For those who don't know, a high 10 is two high fives done at the same time!

◉ When two people face each other for a high five or a high 10, when they jump, have them turn 360 degrees and then do the high five or 10.

2.4   ROLL 'N' GO

8+

The Basics

Roll 'n' Go requires creativity and time on the part of the organizer but once created can be used fairly regularly. Roll 'n' Go gives the appearance of the participants having control of the session and creates a sense of anticipation within the group. Working on a concept similar to that of Monopoly, a team board game is created. Individuals or groups roll the dice, move their piece, and then do whatever is on the board space they land on. In place of Chance and Community Chest cards, create Land Activity and Just for Fun cards. These cards can contain silly games or activities that are very different from those used in the traditional or normal session. Because Roll 'n' Go is usually a highlight of the week, resulting in increased physiological workload due to the high level of enthusiasm, landing in jail is used as a break or an opportunity to get a drink of water. Depending on the level of exertion in the sport, drinking water should also appear on some of the spaces or cards.

How Many Participants?

Two or more.

Land Activity	8 starts	2 x 100 IM	slow & easy 400	JUST FOR FUN	b'stroke pull-kick-kick 200	Rest
200 one-arm freestyle						8 turns
JUST FOR FUN		JUST FOR FUN				200 IM
slow 400 IM		**ROLL 'N GO**				400 your choice
8 x 25 sprints				LAND ACTIVITY		JUST FOR FUN
8 turns						200 kick
Rest	200 pull	JUST FOR FUN	slow & easy 400	4 x 50 sprints	8 starts	Land Activity

This swimming variation of Roll 'n' Go gives participants opportunities for a variety of water-based fitness activities.

What Type of Equipment?

The board game can start as a piece of paper, but as it evolves it should be transferred onto cardboard. If it proves highly popular, laminate it. Depending on the exact type of game created, dice, markers, cards, spin dials, timers, and other objects may be required.

Where?

Anywhere! Roll 'n' Go is ideal for sporting teams of any type, whether the sport takes place on a field, in a gym, in a pool, or on a rink.

Safety Considerations

⊚ If the participants are involved in creating the game, be sure that all activities are suitable for the entire group.

⊚ If it turns out that the workload is getting too high, the leader can assume the omnipotent power of changing certain squares or cards to less strenuous activities, declaring water breaks or rest periods, or both.

Helpful Hints

⊚ You may want to start with a fairly basic game and let it evolve over time. Once the basic concept has been established, the students or athletes may want to extend the existing version or create one of their own. Creating their own version allows them to express their unique group identity.

⊚ Instead of having individuals wait around for their turn, divide the team or class into groups.

Extensions and Variations

If the leader wants a session to focus on, for example, endurance work or technique, the cards used in the game that day can be selected to reflect this.

2.5   RHYTHM RULES!

8+

The Basics

Music can influence people's moods (we have never understood skating rinks that play heavy metal music and then continually ask the skaters to slow down). Music can also be an easily identifiable cue. At the beginning of the session the participants are told that music will either indicate a change in activities or be a cue to stop what they're doing and move to where the coach or teacher is. Although the use of music is not an original idea, we have included it in this chapter to remind people of a simple technique that can literally jazz up a class or session.

How Many Participants?

One or more.

What Type of Equipment?

Tape players and tapes, CD player and CDs, or a talented musician and an instrument. Obviously, if you want an energetic group, play fast-paced music. If you want a relaxing session, play quiet music. The actual music selected should fit the tastes of the participants.

Where?

Anywhere except underwater.

Safety Considerations

For your legal safety, watch out for music copyright laws! In some countries it is illegal to copy music from CD to cassette or from one cassette to another. If you play only cassettes and CDs that you have actually purchased, then there is nothing to worry about. Technically, you may breach copyright laws if you make a compilation tape to play.

Helpful Hints

⑥ Be sure the source of the music is in a place where everyone is able to hear it.

⑥ As a reward for accomplishments or certain behaviors, allow participants to select their favorite music.

Extensions and Variations

Music can easily be incorporated into circuits or station drills where people change activities or stations when the music stops. Prerecorded tapes with blocks of 30 or 60 seconds of music interspersed with 15 seconds of silence are ideal.

Tag Games

Although tag has traditionally been considered a children's game, it can be used effectively with all age groups. Most (if not all) of us have seen children spontaneously initiate games of tag. Although it would be unusual to come across a group of teenagers or adults playing tag, when encouraged by a teacher or coach they, too, enjoy the game of pursuit. For example, a team of male rugby players aged 17 to 21 were lethargic when it came to warming up for practice. The coach revitalized warm-ups through the use of tag games. Any initial signs of reluctance quickly disappeared. In another example, a group of female bocce players aged 26 to 81 willingly and enthusiastically participated in tag games as an effective method of increasing activity.

Simple and generally well-known rules allow tag activities to be set up very quickly, avoiding lengthy periods of explanation. All of the tag games included in this chapter require participation by everyone in the group. We have taken care to avoid exclusionary practices.

Tag games are great for warm-ups or as an energy injector any time. Tag games result in increased heart rates as well as elevated good humor. From our experience, 99.9% of participants immediately jump into a competitive mode and throw themselves wholeheartedly into these activities.

3.1   ALL-IN TAG

8+

The Basics

All-In Tag gets its name from the fact that everyone is in the middle of things from the first second of the game. All-In Tag is probably the quickest game of tag in existence. This game immediately gets everyone involved and creates a flurry of activity. Speed is rarely an advantage, so the quickest individuals may not last the longest. Everyone is It. Once tagged (by anyone), a person must crouch or sit. Being tagged does not exclude a player from the game, however, because everyone is still able to tag others, although once tagged, they cannot leave their spot. If two people tag each other simultaneously, both must crouch or sit.

How Many Participants?

Seven or more.

What Type of Equipment?

Boundary markers.

Where?

Any flat defined area. The size of the area should be restricted so that it is difficult to get across the area without being tagged.

Safety Considerations

⊚ Warning the group to keep their heads up and to remain alert after being tagged can help prevent collisions.

⊚ If athletes are sitting rather than crouching, they are allowed to tag individuals only with their hands (no sticking out feet and tripping people!).

Helpful Hints

With some young groups, individuals tend to get into debates about who tagged whom first. Announce at the beginning of the tag game that if two people cannot agree on who tagged the other first, then both must crouch.

Extensions and Variations

⊚ Increase the challenge by restricting people to forward movement only—no backward steps allowed! You can introduce this variation if there are a few people left who have eluded capture.

⑥ In a pool, this activity can be effective if you have participants practice treading water after they have been tagged. While treading water in one spot, they are still able to tag those who are free.

⑥ With older adults or in confined spaces, substitute walking for running.

3.2   PARTNER TAG

8+

The Basics
In some games of tag, individuals are able to avoid active exercise by hiding in a corner or staying behind other players. Partner Tag requires everyone to be involved the entire time. Everyone finds a partner (see chapter 1). Within each pair, one person is It. Participants try to tag only their own partners. Once a partner is tagged, he or she spins on the spot twice before becoming It and chasing after the partner.

Particularly if you have a small area or more than six individuals, it is important that everyone be restricted to walking; otherwise everyone tends to run into each other while avoiding their partners. Even when restricted to walking, individuals have been known to sweat during this activity!

How Many Participants?
Six or more.

What Type of Equipment?
Boundary markers.

Where?
Any flat defined area.

Safety Considerations
⑥ As mentioned earlier, walking is strongly recommended.

⑥ If you use any of the sport variations, a larger space is needed.

Helpful Hints
⑥ If there is an odd number of people, a group of three can play. Two people can hold hands and play as if they were one person, or within a group of three, the person who is It can chase either of the other

two. Note: it may be better to have everyone in groups of three rather than just all twos and one three. The ability to make quick math computations on the spot is a useful skill!

- To integrate people with physical disabilities into the group, all nondisabled individuals can have their knees tied together with either Velcro straps or nylons. This practice not only helps increase awareness of the effect of movement limitations but also automatically slows the pace of the game.

- If you are asking participants to partner with someone they do not know well, allow time for them to introduce themselves before starting the game. This can be particularly effective in situations where a few new individuals have joined a preestablished group.

Extensions and Variations

- Partners pair up by linking arms and then try to tag another specific pair.

- Instead of spinning on the spot, individuals can do tuck jumps or some other activity that requires little space.

- For sports such as basketball, soccer, or field hockey, athletes can dribble the ball while chasing and being chased.

- For volleyball, athletes can set or pass a ball to themselves while moving.

- In racket sports, individuals can bounce the ball (or the birdie) on their rackets while moving.

3.3   HEADS AND TAILS

8+

The Basics

Heads and Tails is another tag game that involves multiple Its. People can be tagged by almost anyone. The identity of It changes frequently. Participants need to be fully alert and to constantly shift their attention. On the count of three, individuals declare whether they are "heads" or "tails" by placing their hands on the appropriate part of their anatomy. Heads chase tails or tails chase heads. The leader or coach periodically calls out "heads" (meaning heads are It), or "tails" (meaning tails are It). When tagged, the participants become what the person who tagged them was. The aim is for the participants to convert everyone to their own sign (heads or tails). Of course, the leader can determine how close a group can get to total conversion by how she or he times the calls of "heads" and "tails." Participants must keep at least one hand at all times on their head or tail (depending on what they are) so all players can tell what everyone else is.

How Many Participants?
Eight or more.

What Type of Equipment?
Boundary markers.

Where?
Any flat defined area.

Safety Considerations
By having to move with a hand on either one's head or one's behind, a player can rarely attain full speed. However, because many people are moving at once, make sure the area is not too small.

Helpful Hints
- Stipulate that individuals can be tagged only below the neck. In coed situations, you might want to restrict tagging to the back only.

- In any tag game, it is possible to change the boundaries during the game (of course, you need to announce that possibility at the start). Changing the size of the playing field has direct effects on the style of the game. In a larger area, more work is required cardiovascularly; a smaller area requires more agility.

- If most people happen to select the same position, the leader can quickly adopt the opposite position and tag a few people to make the game more balanced.

Extensions and Variations
If the group is evenly divided into two teams, one team is declared to be heads and the other tails. A flip of a coin by the leader determines who will chase whom. The team that is It is then given one minute to convert as many of the opposition as possible by tagging them. Once tagged, individuals should move out of the defined area. Because this is a quick game, people will be out of play for less than 1 minute. The other team should then be given the same opportunity. Unlike the basic version of Heads and Tails where people change identity so often that no one remembers who was what at the start, score can be kept in the team version. Another main difference is that in the basic version, individuals

decide for themselves whether they are going to be a head or a tail at the start of the game. In the team version, two even teams are created and then designated as either heads or tails.

3.4   LINE TAG

8+

The Basics
Line Tag is a game that you probably would not want to use every day; however, this activity can serve as a fresh change of pace. The game follows the basic rules of regular tag except that all players must stay on lines painted on the floor or chalked on the ground. Individuals cannot jump from one line to another but must instead follow a line until it joins another one. Once tagged, a person becomes It. The first It can be either selected by the leader or chosen randomly (see chapter 1).

How Many Participants?
Five or more.

What Type of Equipment?
Lines!

Where?
This activity works best in a gym that has lines painted for multiple sports (e.g., basketball, volleyball, and badminton).

Safety Considerations
Individuals need to keep track of other people as well as the lines, which requires a broad focus of attention. If individuals focus too hard on following the lines, they tend to keep their heads down and then run into other players from behind.

Helpful Hints
- Having the person call out "It" when he or she is tagged makes it obvious to everyone who is It.
- Alternatively, It can hold a ball or some other identifying object.
- Allowing It to tag people within reach regardless of the line on which they stand makes It's life a bit easier.

Extensions and Variations

The variations selected will depend on the skills and abilities of the participants.

⑥ More than one person can be It.

⑥ Requiring individuals to walk toe to heel or to hop slows down the game but helps individuals work on balance. Participants can also be restricted to walking backward.

⑥ In a large area, Line Tag can also be done while dribbling a ball.

3.5   BOPPER TAG

8+

The Basics

The use of a bopper (a light foam bat) revolutionizes the game of tag. The bopper makes a noise when used, allows people to safely vent energy, and brings such a new twist to tag that people fail to associate it with the traditional children's game. Whoever is It has a bopper and tags people by touching them with it anywhere from the waist down. Once someone has been tagged, It drops the bopper, and the person tagged becomes It.

How Many Participants?

Six or more.

What Type of Equipment?

⑥ At least one bopper. Choose for a bopper something that does not hurt a person who is hit with it and that makes a noise when it contacts someone. Inflatable bats or large pieces of compact foam will do the trick. An easy way to create boppers is to cut pool noodles into thirds.

⑥ Boundary markers.

Where?

Any flat defined area.

Safety Considerations

⑥ Although boppers are designed to be safe (and pain-free on contact), it is important to stress that contact should be made below the waist. Alternatively, anywhere below the knees can become the designated "bopper zone." With some groups, demonstrating allowable tags may be useful.

⑥ If using cut pool noodles or pieces of compact foam, be sure no rough edges remain.

Helpful Hints

⑥ Having the leader join in the activity can inspire some participants to put a bit more spirit into it than they might otherwise.

⑥ Using thirds of pool noodles as boppers may seem an extravagant expense at first, but they are durable and last a long time.

Extensions and Variations

⑥ Include more than one bopper and more than one It.

⑥ A bopper can be used in any tag game, so the variations are virtually endless.

⑥ For schools or organizations with strict policies prohibiting human target games, Bopper Tag can be modified. Instead of carrying a bopper, It carries a gator ball (a tough-skinned foam ball). To tag someone, It must touch the person with the gator ball while still holding on to the ball (no throwing). Once a tag has been made, It drops the ball and the person who was tagged becomes It.

3.6   FREEZE AND THAW

8+

The Basics

When people are tagged they freeze, but they can be unfrozen (thawed) by the touch of someone who hasn't yet been tagged. The goal is for the person or people who are It to get everyone frozen at the same time. The number of people who are It depends on how many people are in the group and the size of the playing areas. The "thaw" aspect of this activity encourages individuals to help one another. Instead of each person being interested only in his or her own welfare, Freeze and Thaw incorporates a compassionate aspect.

How Many Participants?

Eight or more.

What Type of Equipment?
Boundary markers.

Where?
Any flat defined area.

Helpful Hints
To make it more obvious which players are frozen, have those who are tagged stand still with their hands on their heads.

Extensions and Variations
- When people are frozen, they stand with their feet shoulder-width apart. The only way a person can be thawed is for someone who hasn't been tagged to crawl between his or her legs. This variation can be used in the shallow end of a pool. To be thawed someone must do a duck dive and swim between the frozen person's legs.

- A leader who wants to develop the participants' strength can use a variety of specified frozen positions, such as the push-up position, a V-sit, or the crab position. Participants required to hold these positions are definitely eager to be thawed!

- Select several "freezers" and several "thawers," leaving the rest of the participants free. The freezers (Its) aim to freeze all the free participants while the thawers try to keep the entire group unfrozen. A ratio of two freezers for every thawer tends to avoid a meltdown.

Safety Considerations (for Variations)
- If participants are asked to adopt positions other than standing (e.g., V-sit or push-up position), it may be safer to ask participants to walk rather than run during the activity.

- Crawling between legs as a method of thawing may best be reserved for games played on grass or in the water.

3.7   LINK TAG

8+

The Basics
Link Tag encourages people to come in contact with almost everyone in a group. People are safe from being tagged when they have linked arms with someone else. There is a maximum of two people per link.

Someone trying to avoid being caught can link onto a preexisting link, forcing the person on the opposite side to let go and become fair game. Two unlinked people are not allowed to form a new link. Linked people must stay stationary. At the start the leader chooses one or more individuals to be It and specifies certain individuals to begin the game unlinked. Once the game begins, the unlinked people can link onto preexisting links. Safety zones allow participants to take a quick breather while still being involved in the game.

How Many Participants?
Twelve or more.

What Type of Equipment?
Boundary markers.

Where?
Any flat defined area.

Safety Considerations
⑥ If one or two individuals are notably slower than the rest, they can become frustrated and somewhat desolate when they continually fail to tag anyone. In this situation the leader can periodically yell "Taggers link up!" Anyone who is It then links arms with a pair, making the person on the opposite side It.

⑥ With arms sliding into other arms, you might recommend that participants remove watches, bracelets, rings, or any other items that may scratch others.

Helpful Hints
⑥ The number of Its and the number of unlinked people at the start depend on group size. As a rough estimate, 10% of the group should be It and 40% of the group should start the game unlinked.

⑥ Because Link Tag is more complex than other forms of tag, it can be useful to have a "walk-through" before the actual game begins.

⑥ If you have a group that is genderphobic (that is, members of the opposite sex are known to have cooties), then links can be formed by touching feet rather than linking arms.

⑥ Individuals with mild physical disabilities may cope better with Link Tag than with other versions of tag because speed is less of an issue and the multiple "safe" options provide rest opportunities.

Extensions and Variations
Adding the rule that each participant can link up with any particular person only once during the activity makes the game more physically and mentally demanding.

3.8   TAIL TAG

8+

The Basics

Each player has a strip of cloth (tail) hanging from the back of his or her shorts. The goal is for each player to collect as many tails as possible. Collected tails are held in the hands. Everyone continues trying to grab tails until they all have been collected. No one may take a tail that has already been collected unless it has been dropped. Tail Tag has the benefit that everyone remains It even after they have had their tail removed, meaning that everyone gets a good workout.

How Many Participants?

Six or more.

What Type of Equipment?

⑥ One strip of cloth (approximately 2 feet long and 2 inches wide) for each participant.

⑥ Boundary markers.

Where?

Any flat defined area.

Safety Considerations

As Tail Tag tends to be a boisterous game, the leader should be attentive to any signs of overly rough play. Having a predetermined signal that indicates that everyone needs to stop comes in handy if contact escalates to an unwanted level.

Helpful Hints

⑥ Long, baggy T-shirts tend to hide the tails. Ask players to tuck in their shirts (even if it isn't fashionable!).

⑥ Stipulate that players are not allowed to hold onto their own tails.

⑥ Having tails be a different color than participants' shorts can be helpful (and can help avoid players unintentionally grabbing the wrong thing).

Extensions and Variations

⑥ Participants carry out the activity while dribbling a ball.

⑥ Participants are allowed to capture tails using only the left (or nonpreferred) hand. With this variation the preferred hand should be placed on the waist.

⑥ If different-colored tails are used, this can become a team game, with each team trying to get as many tails as they can from other teams.

3.9   STICKER TAG

8+

The Basics

This tag game easily moves from individual to team participation. Provide each participant with three stickers. The object is for players to get rid of stickers by sticking them one at a time onto the clothes of others, while avoiding having others put stickers on them. Players who have applied all of their stickers are still in the game, because those who still have stickers will be chasing them. The game continues for a specified time or until everyone has stuck their stickers, whichever comes first. If an outcome is desired, the individual(s) with the fewest stickers stuck on them can be declared the winners. Make sure the following rules are clear from the start:

⑥ No sticking stickers in hair

⑥ No grabbing clothes to slow someone down

⑥ Attach stickers only to the backs of shirts

⑥ Stick only one sticker at a time

How Many Participants?

Three or more.

What Type of Equipment?

⑥ Three stickers for each person.

⑥ Boundary markers.

Where?

Any flat defined area (but not too large!).

Safety Considerations

Enforce rules (e.g., no sticking hair or skin).

Helpful Hints

⑥ Try to find durable stickers that peel off easily and can even be restuck. The labels that movers use to identify the contents of boxes work well.

⑥ Use colored stickers; color can determine team membership.

⑥ Be sure all the stickers are either collected or thrown away before people leave the session or move on to the next activity.

Extensions and Variations

⑥ Players work in pairs to get rid of a combined six stickers. Pair short-armed people with long-armed partners. The first pair to get rid of all their stickers wins.

⑥ Players work as a team. A team is not successful until it has attached all of its stickers onto the other team(s). Individuals cannot remove stickers from themselves; a teammate must remove each sticker before sticking it onto someone from another team(s).

3.10   BALL AND CHAIN

13+

The Basics

Each participant has an inflated balloon tied around an ankle with a piece of string. Individuals tag people by stomping on their balloons to pop them. The last person with an intact balloon wins. All players continue to try to pop other balloons regardless of the status of their own balloon. Be prepared for furious activity, as balloon stomping tends to activate even the most introverted people.

How Many Participants?

Six or more.

What Type of Equipment?

⑥ One (or more) balloons for each person.

⑥ String (approximately 3 feet for each person after tying).

⑥ Boundary markers.

Where?

Indoor areas work best (most outdoor fields contain objects or creatures that can be detrimental to the inflated status of balloons).

Safety Considerations

⑥ A person whose string becomes untied loses the balloon; reaching to save it can result in fingers being stomped.

⑥ If the strings are too short, people are inclined to trip over or pop their own balloons; in addition, it increase the chances of people stomping on others' feet by mistake.

⑥ Be sure to pick up all the balloon carcasses after the game is over.

Helpful Hints

⑥ Try to make the length of the string the same for all players.

⑥ To save your breath, have participants blow up their own balloons.

Extensions and Variations

Ball and Chain easily progresses from an individual to a team situation. Strategies and tactics change as the game evolves:

⑥ Players participate as pairs. They try to protect each other's balloons as they go.

⑥ Players participate as teams, which can be determined by balloon color.

3.11   FREE YOUR FRIENDS

13+

The Basics

Free Your Friends encourages individuals to think of their teammates rather than just themselves. The game invites participants to take risks within a safe environment. Designate one or more players as It. Individuals who are tagged must go to a predetermined detention area. These players can leave the detention area when they are tagged by someone who is still free.

How Many Participants?

Twelve or more.

What Type of Equipment?
Boundary markers, marking out a detention area as well as the general playing field.

Where?
Any large, flat defined area (the larger the area, the more running involved).

Safety Considerations
If circumstances arise where a particular individual is left in detention, introduce a rule that the person who has been detained the longest has to be the first to be freed.

Helpful Hints
Have the group determine what rules should exist in terms of allowing (or not allowing) taggers to guard the detention area against jailbreaks.

Extensions and Variations
⑥ While they are in the detention area, detainees can be required to do sit-ups, skip rope, or perform some other activity.

⑥ Have two teams, each with a separate detention area. Each team tries to get all members of the other team in the detention area.

3.12   CHAIN TAG

8+

The Basics
When It tags someone, the person tagged joins hands with and becomes part of It. Eventually It will be a chain that includes everyone. It can tag people only when completely joined together. Players who are free are not able to go through the middle of the chain or duck under arms. Chain Tag requires teamwork. Teamwork requires effective communication. A variety of individuals may end up in leadership roles during the activity, or a completely democratic and cooperative method of working may evolve. If two or more independent, strong-willed, or bossy individuals are in the group, they will be forced to work together to achieve success.

How Many Participants?
Eight or more.

What Type of Equipment?
Boundary markers.

Where?
Any flat defined area.

Safety Considerations
Remind participants about the "whip" factor—the movement of people in one section of the chain may require even greater speed and distance for those on the end.

Helpful Hints
⑥ Remind individuals of tactics. Tagging a slow person may be easy, but it may hamper successive tags.

⑥ Strongly enforce the rule that if the chain breaks, no one can be tagged. If the chain is tending to break frequently, it may be useful to require the chain to reassemble each time in a predetermined area (e.g., the sidelines), forcing the chain to stop chasing. After everyone has to stop the game once for reassembly, the links tend to get stronger.

Extensions and Variations
⑥ Once a chain has eight people it breaks in half, creating two roving chains of four players each. Alternatively, chains of four can break into two chains of two players each.

⑥ For a great workout, try this activity in the shallow end of a pool.

3.13   TRIANGLE TAG

8+

The Basics
Triangle Tag limits the interaction to a group of four people. Unlike most tag games, Triangle Tag has a strong defensive component. Participants divide into groups of four. Three people hold hands to form a triangle, with one of the three designated as the target. By moving, the other two try to protect that person from the fourth person, who is It. It is not allowed to reach over the triangle but must instead go around the group to tag the target player.

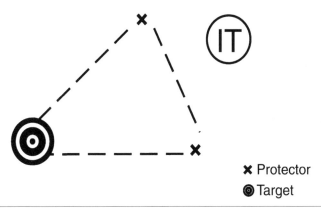

✖ Protector
◉ Target

During Triangle Tag, don't forget to have participants regularly change positions so that everyone gets a chance to run around.

How Many Participants?
Groups of four.

What Type of Equipment?
Boundary markers.

Where?
A flat area that is defined by lines or markers rather than walls (walls tend to be taken advantage of as a method of protecting the target).

Safety Considerations
Strictly enforce the rule that forbids reaching over the triangle.

Helpful Hints
⑤ Setting a time limit (approximately 2 minutes) before changing positions can help keep individuals from becoming too frustrated if they cannot catch their prey. Regularly changing positions also ensures that everyone gets the opportunity to run around.

⑤ If your group does not divide evenly into fours, a fifth person in each group can monitor the time and make sure everyone follows the rules. After 2 minutes everyone changes roles in a predetermined pattern.

Extensions and Variations
⑤ Blindfold the target. This requires the target to completely rely on and trust the two protectors. It also tends to increase the amount and quality of verbal communication. Obviously, this variation makes it simple to include individuals who are visually impaired.

⑥ Have all participants, whether or not they have a physical disability, in wheelchairs.

⑥ Try this game in the shallow end of the pool.

3.14   SPIDERWEB

8+

The Basics
Instead of individuals chasing and being chased, in Spiderweb the players work in groups. The players form groups of three to five. Each group holds hands in a circle. One group is It. It tags another group by brushing up against them. Any kind of light contact of the shoulders, back, hips or arms of any player from the It group qualifies as a tag. Within each group, individuals need to be completely in tune with each other.

How Many Participants?
Nine or more.

What Type of Equipment?
Boundary markers.

Where?
Any flat defined area.

Safety Considerations
⑥ Start this activity at a walking pace. The groups need to learn how to effectively move together before they can increase their speed.

⑥ Participants cannot use their feet to tag, because doing so could lead to tripping.

Helpful Hints
Spiderweb works best when there are four or more groups.

Extensions and Variations
⑥ Identify one member of the group that is It as the tagger. Only when that person brushes up against another group is the other group tagged.

⑥ Have each group link arms with their backs to the center of the circle.

3.15   NOSE AND TOES

8+

● ●

The Basics
Nose and Toes requires participants to alternate between sprinting and balancing. Participants are safe from It when standing on one leg holding the toes of one foot with the opposite side hand and their nose with the other hand. (It would be interesting to see the gymnastics team square off against the track team in this activity!)

How Many Participants?
Five or more.

What Type of Equipment?
Boundary markers.

Where?
Any flat defined area.

If this "safe" position for Nose and Toes isn't challenging enough for your group, check out the variation shown on the next page.

Safety Considerations
Long fingernails are a liability—people may unintentionally scratch themselves when hurriedly grabbing their noses. Leaders should remind those with long fingernails to be careful.

Helpful Hints
Practicing the safe position before the start of the game is important. If a group is having considerable difficulty balancing, then modify the position (e.g., have players stand on one leg and hold the other knee with two hands.

Extensions and Variations

⑤ The arm of the hand holding the nose must go under the knee of the leg in the air.

⑥ Combine Nose and Toes with Freeze and Thaw. When frozen, individuals form the push-up position to make an obvious distinction between who is safe and who is frozen. Reserve this variation for teenagers and adults.

This variation of Nose and Toes is sure to keep your group entertained while giving them practice at balance and agility.

3.16   IT'S IN THE MIDDLE

8+

The Basics

A version of It's in the Middle is a standard activity at skating rinks. With our version, everyone is involved throughout the game. This game works well with large groups. Two or three people are It. On cue, everyone else runs from one end of the field or court to the other. When tagged, individuals become one of the taggers for the next run. Those who avoid being tagged wait at the other end of the field or court until cued to run back. The game continues until everyone is a tagger.

How Many Participants?
Eight or more (the more, the better).

What Type of Equipment?
Boundary markers.

Where?
Any flat defined area.

Safety Considerations
Instruct participants on the etiquette of making painless tags. Restrict tagging to the shoulder or back. It can also be useful to disallow tags that involve slapping or grabbing. With adults, it may be effective to indicate that if the tagger leaves a mark on the taggee, the taggee remains free.

Helpful Hints
For more cardiovascular work, make the end lines further apart.

Extensions and Variations
Have all participants dribble a ball while playing this game.

3.17   OBSTACLE TAG

8+

The Basics
Obstacle Tag requires a broad focus of attention. In addition to being aware of the location of It, individuals also need to be conscious of objects and obstacles on the floor. Begin with a number of objects in the area where the game is played. Anyone who is tagged by It or so much as brushes against one of the objects must sit down and become another obstacle (although one with moving arms). If It touches an obstacle, all previously tagged individuals become free. No running is allowed (running isn't possible if there are enough obstacles in the game).

How Many Participants?
Eight or more.

What Type of Equipment?
⊚ Boundary markers.

⊚ Objects (e.g., skipping ropes, Frisbees, cones).

Where?
Any flat defined area.

Safety Considerations
⊚ Although participants try to avoid stepping on the objects, including objects such as golf balls or marbles can be lethal.

⊚ Having lots of obstacles is actually safer than having only a few; too much space between obstacles encourages participants to run.

Helpful Hints
⊚ Allow yourself time to set up the obstacles.

⊚ If you have more than eight players, begin with more than one person being It.

⊚ This tag game is probably the least energetic form of tag featured in this book. It can therefore serve as a warm-up or cool-down activity.

Extensions and Variations
Instead of having an It, add larger objects to the obstacles. Equipment such as benches, hoops, mats, balance beams, or large cardboard boxes can turn the space into a true obstacle course. In this situation participants move from one end of the area to the other. If they touch something or someone, they then become another obstacle. If everyone can make it across the floor without touching anything, then gradually decrease the amount of time they have to cross, or change the mode of movement. For example, hopping through the course is more difficult than walking.

Ball Tag
Games

Some of the tag games in the preceding chapter can be modified to include ball-handling skills. In this section, however, passing, catching, dribbling, or a combination of these skills is an integral component of each tag game. Even if the sport or activity being taught or coached is not based on ball skills, ball activities can increase motivation, excitement, and purpose. While having fun, participants work on eye-hand coordination as well as fitness.

4.1   PASSING TAG

13+

The Basics

Divide the group into two teams. One team begins with the ball and tries to tag a member of the other team with it. The individual doing the tagging must be holding the ball at the time—no throwing the ball at the other team. To get the ball close to a potential victim, members of the tagging team pass the ball among themselves. Whoever is holding the ball cannot take more than one step. If the ball is dropped, it goes to the other team. Once someone has been tagged, the teams switch roles. Score can be kept. Passing Tag is appropriate for individuals with a range of ball-handling skills. Those who are working on the basics can keep to simple lobs, whereas advanced athletes can incorporate faster or more varied forms of passing such as chest passes, bounce passes, and one-handed passes.

How Many Participants?

Six or more.

What Type of Equipment?

- Boundary markers.
- Pinnies.
- Ball(s).

Where?

Any flat defined area, although it is useful to use a predetermined court or field.

Safety Considerations

If play gets too rough, introduce a rule that only bounce passes are allowed (if playing indoors) or that all passes must be at or below waist height. Bounce passes slow down the game, and lower passes decrease the chance of injury.

Helpful Hints

- Using a larger ball (i.e., a volleyball rather than a tennis ball) makes it easy to tell when someone has been tagged.
- The larger the space, the more tactics required. When the team being chased has lots of room to move, the team with the ball has

to plan how they will manage to get the ball in the hands of a team-mate when the person is within tagging range of the opposition. The more people in a given space (or the smaller the space), the easier it is to make a tag.

Extensions and Variations

⑥ Each team has the ball for a specified time and must tag as many opposing team members as possible within that time. A person cannot be tagged twice in a row. Tagged people continue to be part of the game, as the score is the total number of tags made.

⑥ Instead of using teams, three people start with a ball. Tagged people collect a pinny and become It as well. The game continues until everyone has been tagged (and therefore everyone is It).

⑥ Use more than one ball. This gives the tagging team more chances to make tags but also requires greater awareness from everyone because there is more than one ball to follow.

⑥ Allow the person with the ball to move or to run. Instead of being restricted to one step, the player with the ball can chase the opposition while holding the ball.

⑥ To increase the difficulty of the game, stipulate that players can use only one hand to catch and throw the ball. This variation is appropriate for advanced athletes only.

4.2   HELP ME TAG

8+

The Basics

Help Me Tag is a good introductory activity because it requires partici-pants to know each other's names. The more names individuals know, the more options they have. This game is not particularly demanding physically. Have enough balls for approximately one-third of the group. The person who is It tries to tag the other players; individuals are safe from being tagged when holding a ball. The only way to get a ball is to ask a person politely by name (e.g., "Chris, please pass me the ball."). The person must pass the ball when asked correctly. If the ball is dropped, it is taken out of the game. The number of Its can vary. When people are tagged they become It. Similarly, an It who tags someone becomes free. The game should be played for a specified length of time.

How Many Participants?
Nine or more.

What Type of Equipment?
⑥ Boundary markers.

⑥ Approximately one ball for every three people.

Where?
Any flat defined area.

Safety Considerations
To keep the game on the more sedate side, require that all passes be made underhand.

Helpful Hints
⑥ If small balls are used, some crafty individuals may try to conceal the fact that they are in possession of one. Stipulate that the balls must be readily visible at all times.

⑥ If the group is newly formed, encourage participants to spend a minute or two to learn each other's names before starting the game. Once a class or a team knows each other, this game has limited use.

⑥ Anyone with the ability to catch, throw, hear, and speak can participate in this game. Paraplegic individuals and those with mild cerebral palsy can easily be integrated.

Extensions and Variations
⑥ Have It carry an easily identifiable object. Once someone has been tagged, It drops the object for the new It to pick up. This variation makes the identity of It clear to everyone.

⑥ Use balls with a variety of weights (e.g., a jelly ball or medicine ball, a Ping-Pong ball, a basketball, and a foam ball). The varied weights require greater attention when it comes to throwing and catching.

4.3   THIEVES

13+

The Basics

All but a few players have balls that they dribble. The players without balls are thieves and try to steal a ball from someone else. Once a ball is stolen, the player who lost it tries to steal someone else's. The game continues for a specified length of time. Thieves is a very skill-oriented game. Advantages include constant participation for everyone (no one has to wait around for their turn), multiple ball contacts, and the opportunity for participants to practice ball-handling skills without worrying about keeping score or embarrassing themselves in the spotlight. Critiquing others' performances is the last thing on anyone's mind, because everyone is concentrating on maintaining control of their own balls. As a result, individuals with less ability can easily practice their stealing skills without anyone judging them.

How Many Participants?

Three or more.

What Type of Equipment?

6 Balls (slightly fewer than the number of people).

6 Boundary markers.

Where?

A flat defined area. It's easiest if you use a predefined court or field.

Safety Considerations

Individuals always need to be alert for stray balls.

Helpful Hints

If things get too chaotic with large numbers participating at the same time, you can divide the participants into smaller groups. If a discrepancy in skill level results in certain individuals never having the ball, break into smaller groups based on skill level.

Extensions and Variations

6 A variety of forms of dribbling can be used. Thieves can be effective in field hockey, ice hockey, basketball, and soccer.

6 For volleyball, tennis, or badminton, the dribbling can be aerial (e.g., the players can pass the ball themselves or bounce the ball or birdie off their own rackets).

4.4   PROTECT YOUR TURF

13+

The Basics

Each player stands next to an upright cone or plastic soft drink bottle. Players throw balls at the other players' cones or bottles, trying to knock them down while protecting their own to keep it upright. Once their object has been knocked over, players can continue to attack others, but they cannot replace their object. To begin the game, cones or bottles can be placed in a circle or in triangles, always with one person next to each cone or bottle. Each individual plays offense and defense at the same time. If you want to see a rapid flurry of activity, this is the game to choose!

How Many Participants?

Two or more.

What Type of Equipment?

⑥ One cone or plastic soft drink bottle per person.

⑥ A minimum of one ball per person.

⑥ Predetermined location for each cone or bottle.

Where?

Inside a gym works best as less time is needed to chase and retrieve balls.

Safety Considerations

If balls are coming from too many directions at once, break the participants into small groups (triangles with three individuals or even one-on-one).

Helpful Hints

⑥ Be sure that everyone is equal distance from a wall. It is a definite disadvantage to have to leave the object to run a long distance to retrieve a ball.

⑥ A little sand or water in the bottom of a plastic soft drink bottle makes it much more stable.

⑥ If the game stalls because participants are unwilling to leave their object to collect balls, stipulate that points are accrued by knocking over other people's objects.

✗	Player
△	Cone
○	Ball

Starting position for Protect Your Turf. This game allows players to play both offense and defense at the same time.

Extensions and Variations

◎ Instead of everyone playing as individuals, divide the group into two teams, each with the same number of targets to protect. Each team can decide for itself the strategy it uses. For example, everyone can continue to play both offense and defense, or the team can designate specific players to perform specific tasks, such as offense, defense, or ball collection.

◎ Instead of throwing, dribble the ball and then kick or shoot it (e.g., for field hockey or soccer players).

◎ Use containers of water instead of cones or bottles. The aim is to keep all of the water in your container and knock out the water in everyone else's. (Plastic ice cream containers or small plastic buckets are perfect.) If using this variation, move the game outside (unless you have an incredibly understanding custodial staff!).

8+

4.5   BALL PAIR TAG

The Basics

Divide the group into pairs. Partners stand next to each other and link arms. The leader selects one pair to be It. Each person in the It pair has a free hand. It is given two balls, one for each free hand. The balls need to be extremely soft. The It pair makes a tag by hitting another pair with a ball. Once a tag is made, It must drop the other ball, if they still have one. The pair that was tagged becomes It, collects the two balls, and begins the chase. Play Ball Pair Tag for a specified length of time.

How Many Participants?
Six or more.

What Type of Equipment?
Two soft balls that people wouldn't mind getting hit with. Try foam balls (Nerf balls) or fleece balls.

Where?
Any flat defined area, although it is useful to use a predefined court or field.

Safety Considerations
Leaders should test the softness of any balls to be used. Their softness can be demonstrated by allowing the participants to throw the balls at the coach or teacher (if school policy permits).

Helpful Hints
⑥ Give pairs a minute or two to discuss the strategy they will use if and when they become It. For example, it would be silly for a pair made up of a left-handed person and a right-handed person to play with their throwing arms linked.

⑥ Remind pairs that if they throw their two balls and miss, they need to remain linked while they collect the balls.

Extensions and Variations
⑥ Have more than one pair as It.

⑥ Increase the difficulty of the game by tying together the knees or ankles of each pair as in a three-legged race.

⑥ Stipulate a no-talking rule. Each pair needs to figure out another method of communicating with each other about the direction in which they are going to move.

⑥ For schools or organizations with a strict policy against human target games, Ball Pair Tag can be modified by stipulating that balls cannot be thrown. A tag can only be made if It is still holding the ball. In this version, be sure to have more than one pair as It.

Individual Challenges

Individual challenges are physical activities that entertainingly test the individual and can take place with any number of participants. These are quick fillers you can slot into a spare few minutes while equipment is being set up or group drills are delayed for some reason.

Individual challenges are just that—challenges for the individual. Each participant should work on bettering his or her own performance rather than comparing it to the performance of others. Regular inclusion of individual challenges can encourage individuals to monitor their own performances, set goals, and see evidence of improvement.

As comparisons are made only to oneself, individuals with a variety of disabilities can easily be included in most of the activities in this section. Use common sense when selecting activities for particular individuals.

5.1 LOFTY LEAPS

8+

The Basics
It's time to imitate a kangaroo! Challenge your athletes to jump and reach as high as they can from a standing start. Height can be recorded in a number of ways. You can assign each individual his or her own rope that remains tied to a balcony or beam. Once the individual succeeds in touching it four times out of five, then half an inch is cut off the rope. Another alternative is to measure off a space on the wall from about 5 feet to 9 feet, depending on participants' height and jumping skill. Individuals use chalk on their fingers to mark their standing reach and then their jumping reach. The difference between the two marks is their jump height.

How Many Participants?
One or more.

What Type of Equipment?
A wall with height noted in half inches or centimeters, or one piece of rope (and a place to tie it) for each person.

Where?
Anywhere with a markable wall or a place to hang rope.

Safety Considerations
Emphasize that these are standing jumps—no approach allowed.

Helpful Hints
- Having individual ropes or other indicators to note personal jumping height is more motivating to athletes than just marking a wall and then measuring the height of the jump.
- Because this is an individual activity, anyone who can jump can participate (the only exception might be a double-arm amputee). Individuals who are visually impaired can get immediate feedback on the height of their jumps using the rope version of this activity (obviously, they need to be shown where the rope is).

Extensions and Variations
For working on muscular endurance, have each individual jump 10 times in 1 minute, recording only the lowest jump.

5.2   DARE TO BE DIZZY

13+

The Basics

Figure skaters and springboard divers may be able to spin circles around participants from other sports in Dare to Be Dizzy. Participants place the palm of a hand on the floor, bend the knees, and then move the body around the hand until their feet come back to where they started. If you keep score, this full circle will count as 1. See how many revolutions each person can do in 15 to 30 seconds.

How Many Participants?

One or more.

What Type of Equipment?

No equipment needed!

Where?

Indoors works best. Dry grass works reasonably well, too.

Safety Considerations

⑥ When participants first try this activity, begin with a time limit of 15 seconds. Very few people get dizzy that quickly.

⑥ If more than one person is doing this activity at the same time, be sure participants are spaced far enough apart so that if someone gets dizzy and loses their balance or sense of direction, collisions do not occur.

Helpful Hints

⑥ Using an existing line on the floor as a reference point for the start and finish of each circle makes counting easier.

⑥ Be sure participants keep their eyes open. Closing them increases the dizziness factor.

⑥ Try Dare to Be Dizzy moving in both directions.

⑥ People with mild physical disabilities (such as mild cerebral palsy) are able to do this activity. Single-limb amputees are also capable of participating (arm amputees are obviously able to spin only on one side; leg amputees can hop or shuffle as they spin around). As with all of the activities in this section, no one is comparing people with each other, so all individuals are able to challenge themselves.

Extensions and Variations

Find two lines 10 feet apart (e.g., the attack line and the center line on a volleyball court). Participants stand between the two lines. They then touch each line with the same hand, turning in the same direction at all times by pivoting on the non-lunging foot. See how many touches each participant can achieve in 30 seconds. This variation is an excellent activity for sports where you want people to be able to be low when they move (e.g., volleyball or squash). Because athletes are moving within a space of 10 feet, dizziness is not much of an issue.

5.3   ROCK AND ROLL

18+

The Basics

Rock and Roll is challenging and suitable only for experienced athletes or regular exercisers. Participants should be capable of completing 15 regular push-ups with good form before trying this activity. Each individual wheelbarrows with a ball. Individuals form the push-up position with their hands on a ball. Keeping their hands on the ball and the legs and body straight, they attempt to move forward. The goal is to go as far as possible without the ball rolling out from under the hands resulting in a face plant.

Individuals should be capable of completing 15 regular push-ups with good form before participating in Rock and Roll.

How Many Participants?
One or more.

What Type of Equipment?
One large ball (basketball or bigger) or medicine ball for each person. Golf balls are extremely challenging, or should we say impossible! Ping-Pong balls can't cope with the pressure!

Where?
Indoors.

Safety Considerations
Participants may want to begin this activity on mats. Hard floors may discourage all but the strongest and most skilled athletes.

Helpful Hints
- ⑥ Encourage people to stay in the push-up position. Because this activity is difficult, participants tend to try alternate positions.
- ⑥ Placing the hands slightly behind the ball can facilitate forward progress a bit.
- ⑥ Participants who are visually impaired can try this activity if given sufficient direction and space. (We say "try" because not all fit, sighted individuals are able to perform this activity successfully!)

Extensions and Variations
Rock and Roll is challenging enough by itself—no variations necessary.

8+

5.4   ROLL UP

The Basics
Although some people will measure Roll Up success in millimeters, others (e.g., rhythmic gymnasts) will measure success in feet. Participants lie on their stomachs with their heads toward the wall, arms straight, and hands above the head. They then roll a ball up the wall with their hands. The aim is to get the ball as high as possible while keeping both hands on it. Anyone who is capable of holding the initial position with the ball 1 millimeter off the floor is able to do this activity.

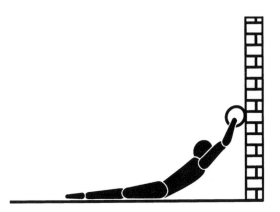

The aim of Roll Up is to get the ball as high up the wall as possible while holding it with both hands.

How Many Participants?
One or more.

What Type of Equipment?
⑥ One ball for each person (volleyballs work well).

⑥ A wall.

Where?
Indoors, preferably on a clean floor!

Safety Considerations
⑥ Stipulate that individuals must be able to hold their final position—no jerking up to a momentary high. Stress that all movement must be slow and controlled.

⑥ Avoid using jelly balls or medicine balls.

Helpful Hints
When tracking multiple results for an individual, be sure he or she uses the same type of ball each time.

Extensions and Variations
Participants lie on their stomachs with their feet toward the wall, holding the ball between their feet. Once again, they aim to get the ball as high as possible. Be sure participants keep their knees straight! To reduce back pressure, have participants keep their arms at their sides.

5.5 NO ELEPHANTS ALLOWED

8+

The Basics
The elephant is the only mammal that cannot jump; therefore elephants are not capable of doing this activity! In No Elephants Allowed, the goal is to cover as much distance forward as possible with each jump. Locate two lines between 30 and 60 feet apart. Participants stand at the first line with feet together. Keeping the feet together, each person does a standing broad jump, then continues jumping until he or she crosses the second line. Individuals must begin each successive jump in the position in which they finished the previous jump. No one is allowed to take extra steps or to shuffle or straighten their feet. If individuals lose their balance and fall, they need to start over from the beginning.

How Many Participants?
One or more.

What Type of Equipment?
Line markers.

Where?
A volleyball court is perfect—the lines are already there. Otherwise, use a flat, nonslippery surface.

Safety Considerations
Due to the explosive nature of this activity, participants should stretch before beginning No Elephants Allowed (particularly their quadriceps).

Helpful Hints
- Remind participants to let their arms help propel them.
- To include individuals in wheelchairs, equate one push with one jump.

Extensions and Variations
- Instead of having participants cover a specific distance, specify a number of jumps (e.g., eight). How much distance can each person cover with the specified number of jumps?
- To really work on balance, blindfold the participants.
- Try it hopping on one foot!

13+

5.6 CIRCLE WALK

The Basics

People often complain that they feel as though they are going around in circles. In Circle Walk, this is a sign of success. Participants get into the push-up position. Keeping their feet in one spot, they walk their hands around in a circle, pivoting around their feet. The objective is to see how many times they can make it around in 1 minute. Because participants don't need to react to things going on around them, this is a suitable activity for individuals who are visually impaired.

How Many Participants?

One or more.

What Type of Equipment?

No equipment needed!

Where?

A flat, clean area.

Safety Considerations

ⓖ Be sure participants keep their backsides down—the shoulders should be the highest point. Leaders should keep an eye on form. When form breaks down, dictate a rest or a change in activity.

ⓖ For novice exercisers, simply holding the push-up position without moving is challenge enough.

Helpful Hints

ⓖ Have each individual complete the task twice, once in each direction.

ⓖ People get better at Circle Walk with practice. Don't let participants give up after just one attempt.

Extensions and Variations

ⓖ Time how long it takes participants to complete two circles.

ⓖ For a serious challenge, ask participants to flip over. They continue to walk their hands around their feet but do so with their stomachs facing the ceiling. Be sure they keep their bodies straight and don't let their backsides sag! Ensure that participants are capable of completing two full circles in the standard position before having them try this variation.

It's important to keep proper position (top figure) while performing the Circle Walk.

Team Challenges

This chapter differs from the others in that the emphasis is not on physical skills but rather the opportunity for participants to develop their mental, emotional, and social skills. Sometimes, in the hectic rush of trying to cover a certain amount of material or preparing a team for competition, teachers and coaches can forget the importance of these nonphysical skills. However, without cohesion, communication, trust, and cooperation, the group is unlikely to perform well and certainly will be less likely to enjoy the sessions. If people do not feel this sense of belonging and affiliation with others, they are likely to drop out of the group. The activities in this chapter are designed to encourage a sense of belonging. In other words, these activities encourage group collaboration with cooperative team tasks.

We encourage teachers and coaches to use these activities to invite participants to make connections between the activity and real-life situations. With the help of guided discussion, participants can begin to transfer some of the skills they've learned in the activity to other settings.

Lighthearted game situations can often encourage people to discuss topics that they might otherwise ignore or that might lead to bickering and confrontation. Capitalize on this.

Following are several reflection suggestions:

1. "Tell me what happened."

2. "Line up, close your eyes, take a step forward if you feel the team worked well together; take a step back if you feel the team could have worked better together. Open your eyes. Tell me why you are standing in that position."

3. During short segments, write down a verbatim transcript of what participants say while they are in action. Sometimes when you repeat these quotes to the participants, they are able to identify behavioral patterns on their own.

This chapter follows a sequence from simple activities involving basic cooperation skills to more challenging activities that require considerable trust and responsibility. The creation of a supportive environment is essential. If a group is not demonstrating the essential skills needed to create an emotionally and physically safe environment, the facilitator should not allow the group to move on to a more challenging activity and should perhaps backtrack.

6.1   HAVE YOU EVER...?

8+

The Basics

Have You Ever...? is an ideal activity to conduct when a group is first getting to know each other. The goal is for participants to learn things about each other that they would not normally think to ask. They learn that there is more to their classmates or teammates than the fact that they play a particular position or run a particular distance in a particular time.

Create a circle using hoops or some other markers. Have one fewer hoop or marker than there are people. Each participant then stands inside a hoop or on a marker, facing the center of the circle, except for the person without a hoop or marker, who goes in the middle. The center person asks a question that begins with, "Have you ever..." Examples could be, "Have you ever jumped out of an airplane?" "Have you ever broken a bone?" "Have you ever lived in another country?" The possibilities are endless. The only restriction is that the question must reflect something that the person in the center has actually done. All the participants standing around the circle who can honestly answer yes to the question must leave their spot, move inside the circle, and then quickly try to find another spot vacated by someone else. The person who asked the question also tries to find a vacant spot. No one is allowed to just switch places with the person next to them. The person who is unable to find a vacant spot remains in the middle and asks the next question. If no one can answer yes to the question, the person in the middle asks another question.

How Many Participants?
Six to 15 in each group.

What Type of Equipment?
Hoops or markers (one fewer than there are people).

Where?
Any flat space.

Safety Considerations
⑤ When rushing across the circle, participants need to keep an eye out for others doing the same thing.

⑤ Before the activity begins, stipulate that no potentially embarrassing questions are allowed.

Helpful Hints
⑤ If two people claim a space at the same time, both go into the center and ask a question jointly.

⑤ If participants do not know each other's names, have them state their own name before asking a question.

⑤ Making a larger circle gives the person in the middle a greater chance of finding a spot and provides some exercise for everyone.

Extensions and Variations
At camps or other indoor situations where the emphasis is not on physical activity, you can use chairs in place of hoops or markers. Make sure chairs are sturdy and do not have arms. As in the game of musical chairs, the chairs sometimes take a beating in this activity.

6.2   PRETZELS

8+

The Basics

Pretzels, sometimes known as Knots, is a useful activity for focusing on cooperation and verbal communication. Because the solution to the problem is never the same twice, this activity encourages participants to focus on process. Participants stand in a circle, facing each other. Each person extends one hand into the middle of the circle and grasps someone else's hand. Each person then reaches out with the other hand and grasps another hand, so the entire circle has become a massive pretzel. It is imperative that each person holds the hands of two different people. The aim of the group is to untangle the pretzel while staying linked. Usually this results in a circle of people holding hands, but sometimes two circles result. Some people may be facing into the circle and others away from it.

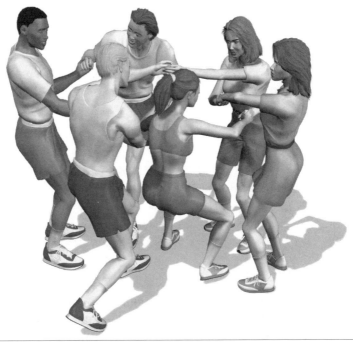

Pretzels is a great activity for improving cooperation and communication—the group can't become untangled without working together.

How Many Participants?
Five to 12 people in each group.

What Type of Equipment?
No equipment needed!

Where?
Anywhere!

Safety Considerations
Be sure all movements to disentangle are done smoothly and slowly. If a section of the pretzel suddenly has a brainstorm about how to untangle themselves, their quick movements may force another part of the pretzel into extremely uncomfortable, even painful, positions.

Helpful Hints
⊚ Pretzels can be a great activity for a group that might be developing factions or cliques. Using the activities from chapter 1 (Activities for Splitting Into Groups) allows the creation of random groups.

⊚ If the group is newly formed, require that by the time everyone untangles themselves, they must know each other's names.

⊚ Although not a particularly successful activity for individuals in wheelchairs, Pretzels needs virtually no adaptation for individuals with impaired hearing or vision or who have a mild intellectual or physical disability.

Extensions and Variations
⊚ Allow only nonverbal communication (no talking).

⊚ Have participants do the activity blindfolded (it's challenging but possible!).

6.3   FIND IT FAST

8+

The Basics
Find It Fast is one of the few team challenges that requires lots of running. Find It Fast is also demanding for the leader in that setting it up requires time and effort. The good news is that the time and effort are

always worthwhile—every group with whom we have worked has thrown themselves wholeheartedly into the activity. Give each team a scavenger list of questions. The teams must find the answers by moving to different locations. Some examples could be, "How many trees are at the top of the hill behind the softball diamond?" "Which staircase in the school has 22 steps?" "What is the third letter of the second word of the sign on the east wall of building X?" "How many vents are there in the gym?" and "What color is the pole of the highest light on the football field?"

The team must stay together at all times. A time limit is given (e.g., 15 minutes). All teams must report back at the end of that time, signaled by a whistle or bell. The goal is for each team to collect as many pieces of information as possible.

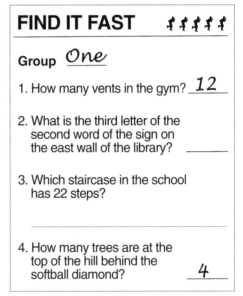

FIND IT FAST

Group *One*

1. How many vents in the gym? _12_

2. What is the third letter of the second word of the sign on the east wall of the library? _____

3. Which staircase in the school has 22 steps?

_____

4. How many trees are at the top of the hill behind the softball diamond? _4_

Be sure your group has safe access to the facilities that you include on your Find It Fast cards.

How Many Participants?
Any number from two pairs to 10 groups of seven.

What Type of Equipment?
⑥ Cards or lists containing the questions.

⑥ Pencils (one for each group).

Where?
Usually outdoors. It is ideal to have access to a school campus or a camp area.

Safety Considerations
Avoid areas where traffic or other hazards (e.g., a vicious neighborhood dog) may be located.

Helpful Hints

⑥ If using a location that other groups also use, make sure that Find It Fast will not disrupt other activities.

⑥ Award bonus points for questions that are more difficult than others (e.g., the answers are less obvious or found further away).

⑥ If you have many groups, it is helpful to vary the order of the questions on the lists.

⑥ Groups that return late lose credit for one question for every minute they are late.

⑥ For groups that don't know each other very well, include a task requiring that each group member learn a unique fact about each other group member. With the time pressure of Find It Fast, they need to acquire this knowledge on the run.

Extensions and Variations

⑥ Create a word or sentence. At each location that correctly provides the answer to a question, the group finds a letter or a word. Once they have collected all of them, the group unscrambles the letters to form a word or the words to form a sentence.

⑥ Instead of providing a list of questions at the beginning, have each group return to a rendezvous station to pick up each successive question. This allows the leader to monitor the progress of groups.

6.4   SEE NO OBSTACLES

13+

The Basics

See No Obstacles requires a combination of trust and effective nonverbal communication. Divide the participants into groups of approximately four. Ask one member of each group to go to the facilitator to receive instructions. These volunteers are told that they are the leaders of their groups but can communicate only by touch. The leaders' objective is to guide their blindfolded teams around an obstacle course as safely and as quickly as possible. When the leaders return to their groups, they tell the others that they are going to complete an obstacle course while blindfolded but that all instruction will be tactile. Tactile does not mean physically leading the group, or physically placing their feet in the appropriate places. Rather, a tap on the right shoulder might mean turn to the right, whereas a light touch on the head might mean take a step forward. Allow the groups a few minutes to determine their tactile code. The group members then put on their blindfolds and the activity begins. At the end of the activity the teacher or coach should lead a discussion. Topics could include the impact of planning, the importance of trust, and the role of different forms of communication.

How Many Participants?
Groups of three or four.

What Type of Equipment?
⑤ Obstacles (e.g., uneven terrain, steps, chairs, trees, balance beams, mats, or benches).

⑤ Blindfolds (three for every four people).

Where?
Indoors or outdoors.

Safety Considerations
⑤ Be sure that the leaders are aware of all potential obstacles.

⑤ Inform followers that if they feel unsafe, they can stop until they receive more effective guidance.

Helpful Hints
Blindfolds can easily be made from old sheets or, better yet, stretchy material. For frequent flyers, blindfolds can be obtained on overnight international flights. Every passenger gets one, but 90% of the blindfolds are left behind on the plane. Either stay behind and clean up after the passengers leave or be assertive and ask for them as passengers disembark. Be sure to regularly wash blindfolds.

Extensions and Variations
⑤ Allow each group leader the use of four sounds: "umm," "ipp," "bonk," and "bip" (the participants can change the particular sounds). "Umm" means move forward, "ipp" means stop, "bonk" means turn right, and "bip" means turn left. Once the group has started the obstacle course, only the designated sounds can be used (no more touches). Each group should create its own auditory signals, because if everyone uses the same signals the end result is mass confusion.

⑤ If anyone in a group touches an obstacle, the entire group must return to the start of the course.

6.5   BLINDFOLD RUN

18+

The Basics
Trust in teammates can be slow to develop but easily broken. Therefore activities such as Blindfold Run should be introduced only when you are confident that the group is mature enough to provide the emotional and physical support necessary to create a safe environment for all individuals. Establish a straight running course between 50 and 100 feet long. A blindfolded volunteer stands at the beginning of the run and is challenged to run as fast as he or she can to the other end, trusting the physical presence and the voice cues of team members to protect him or her from any harm. Place several people around the edges of the running course. Be sure to have a number of people at least 20 feet before the end of the course. When the runner gets to this point, these people let him or her know that the sprint is over; the space allows the runner to slow down and stop before the end of the course.

How Many Participants?
Seven or more.

What Type of Equipment?
One blindfold.

Where?
A flat, straight, obstacle-free area at least 50 feet long.

Safety Considerations
Remind all participants that runners are to challenge themselves but are not to push too far past their comfort zone.

Helpful Hints
- People become more confident with practice, so everyone should have at least two turns as the runner. It may be useful to let people run once without the blindfold to familiarize themselves with the terrain.
- Have a designated individual at the end of the course to provide the main verbal cues (e.g., "go, go, go" and "stop"). It is helpful if this person has a strong voice. The other participants around the course provide security by their physical presence, but only speak if the runner is veering off course towards them.

Extensions and Variations

Include the sprint start (starting from a crouch position). The change in head angle affects the runner's balance and kinesthetic awareness.

6.6   THE BARRICADE

13+

. . . .

The Basics

The Barricade combines trust, reaction time, and speed. The entire group is responsible for reacting in time to maintain the safety of everyone involved. No equipment is needed, so no set-up time is required. Position team members in two lines facing each other, with sufficient distance between the lines so that the participants' outstretched arms just touch. This position (with hands touching) forms the barricade. A volunteer stands facing the end of the two lines, far enough away to be able to achieve close to maximum running speed by the time he or she reaches the lines. The collective responsibility of the lines is to raise or drop their arms a split second before the runner reaches them. The runner continues to run at maximum speed until all people have been passed. For consistency, the group should decide beforehand whether to raise or drop their arms. Arms go up (or down) as the runner reaches each individual team member.

Everyone in the group needs to be attentive to the runner to achieve success in the Barricade.

How Many Participants?

Seven or more (although 21 to 25 are ideal). A greater number of people provides a greater sense of a barricade and therefore a greater sense of accomplishment when the runner maintains speed.

What Type of Equipment?

No equipment needed!

Where?

Any flat area free of obstacles or gravel. Be sure to allow for some space at the end of the lines for slowing down and stopping!

Safety Considerations

It is imperative that everyone focus on the runner before he or she starts. Some signal should be selected to indicate the start.

Helpful Hints

Start with a practice walk-through to ensure that everyone completely understands the structure of the activity.

Extensions and Variations

By changing the distance between the two lines, you can alter the perceived difficulty of the activity. For example, if the lines touch clenched fists instead of fingertips, the task is perceived to be more intimidating. To make the task even more intimidating, position the lines closer together so that participants' arms actually overlap. Also, having thumbs pointing up creates a greater sense of a barricade.

6.7   PENDULUM

13+

The Basics

Divide the participants into groups of three, with all members of a group approximately the same size (you can use Size Systems [activity 1.3] for dividing the group). Ask for a volunteer in each group to stand as straight and stiff as a board, feet together with arms crossed over the chest. The other two participants, the catchers, stand on either side of the volunteer, with one foot pressed up against the side of the volunteer's foot and the other foot back (approximately 3 feet) to provide a stable base. The catchers hold the volunteer by the shoulders and gently begin to rock that person from side to side. At the request of the volunteer they can either continue to maintain contact with the shoulders at all times or release their hold on the shoulders as they push the person from side to side. The volunteer can also ask the catchers to move apart so the distance he or she falls gradually increases. Pendulum is a great starting point or lead-up to many trust activities, particularly those that require the lifting of participants.

Starting position

Catchers farther apart

How Many Participants?
Groups of three.

What Type of Equipment?
No equipment needed!

Where?
Any nonslip surface.

Pendulum is a great lead-up to many trust activities—communication and concentration are important.

Safety Considerations

⑥ The volunteer in the center is always in charge and must ask "Catchers ready?" to which the catchers must answer "Ready" before the volunteer starts falling. It is always the center person's choice whether he or she wishes to remain at the current level of movement or asks the catchers to move apart.

⑥ If you notice participants joking or ridiculing each other, such as groaning or making comments when a heavier person is in the center, you must stop the activity. Address this issue before commencing the activity by discussing the genuine appreciation of individual differences. Even people who appear to be emotionally tough and immune to criticism can be devastated by a careless comment.

⑥ You must also stop the activity if the catchers either pretend not to catch or actually fail to catch the person in the middle. In this scenario discuss how quickly trust can be lost. The person in the middle needs to have complete trust in the catchers. Once trust is lost, it may take the group weeks or even months to regain it. Even if a catcher is only "kidding around," the result is the same as if the catcher had absolutely no concern for the volunteer's safety.

⑥ Never force anyone to be the center person.

Helpful Hints

Some groups have performed this activity with the center person facing one catcher and with his or her back to the other. This can potentially create some problems—for example, a participant may feel discomfort at being face-to-face with someone at such close proximity, or the person in the center may inadvertently (despite the crossed arms) be touched on the breast. Also, requiring one foot to be pressed up against the side of the center person's foot creates a naturally stable position and a feeling of safety. Therefore, always have the volunteer face forward with the catchers on either side.

Extensions and Variations

Blindfold the person in the middle.

6.8   BLOWING IN THE BREEZE

13+

The Basics

This activity is an extension of Pendulum; it involves trusting a group rather than just two people. Instead of having only two catchers, a group of five to nine catchers form a circle around the volunteer. The catchers then move the center person across and around the circle rather than simply back and forth as in Pendulum. The experience is enhanced when the person in the middle closes his or her eyes.

How Many Participants?

Groups of 6 to 10.

What Type of Equipment?

No equipment needed!

Where?

A dry, clean space, either indoors or outdoors on a lawn.

Safety Considerations

⊚ Make sure that participants in the circle are spaced according to their strength so the circle can provide balanced support.

⊚ Never force anyone to be the center person.

Helpful Hints

⑥ Remind the person in the center to keep his or her arms folded across the chest.

⑥ Remind catchers to maintain a balanced position at all times.

Extensions and Variations

Autumn Leaves: on a nonverbal signal from a predetermined catcher, the group lifts the center person to a horizontal position at approximately the shoulder height of the group. In complete silence, the group then rocks the center person gently back and forth. While rocking, the group slowly lowers the lifted person to the ground. Ask the group to always designate who will be holding the head and the heavier sections of the body. In addition, encourage participants to keep a straight back when lowering the person by maintaining eye contact with the person across from them. This keeps the lifters' heads up and discourages bending their backs. Reserve Autumn Leaves for older teenagers and adults.

6.9   CATCH ME!

18+

The Basics

This activity is sometimes referred to as Trust Fall. Do not let your group attempt Catch Me! until they have first successfully completed the Autumn Leaves variation of Blowing in the Breeze. A volunteer stands on a desk, tree stump, or other object approximately 3 feet high. The rest of the group stands below the volunteer in two lines with arms outstretched, ready to catch the volunteer. Rather than the two lines meeting fingertip to fingertip, people alternate their arms so the entire space is full of arms, not just fingers or hands. A useful guide is to have fingertips touching the elbows of the participants in the opposite line. The volunteer stands with his or her back to the group with arms crossed in front. The volunteer says, "Ready, catchers?" to which the catchers reply, "Ready." The volunteer then says, "Falling" just before slowly leaning backward. The catchers then catch! The faller must keep a straight and stiff body the entire time. After the faller is securely caught, the catchers slowly lower his or her feet to the ground so the volunteer is once again standing.

Catch Me! participants should be careful to interlock arms to create a sturdy platform for catching.

How Many Participants?
Nine to 13 people in each group.

What Type of Equipment?
⑥ Something to stand on (e.g., chair, table, tree stump).

⑥ Mats are optional. Although mats give the appearance of increased safety and security, in reality that may not be the case. When using mats, the catchers may be a little less vigilant, thinking that the mats will protect the person falling. In addition, the catchers' footing may be less stable when they are standing on mats.

Where?
A grassy area outdoors or a gym floor indoors. Avoid concrete floors!

Safety Considerations
⑥ Offer a variety of heights to accommodate a range of risk-taking behaviors, but never allow a height that is higher than the catchers' shoulders.

⑥ All participants must be alert at all times. Stop the activity at any signs of distraction or inattentiveness.

Helpful Hints
The faller needs to keep a completely straight and stiff body. Participants practice this position in Pendulum, Blowing in the Breeze, and Autumn Leaves. This body position helps to distribute the weight evenly across all of the catchers.

Extensions and Variations
Blindfold the person falling; doing so often makes him feel as if he is falling farther.

6.10   MINEFIELD

13+

The Basics

Scatter a variety of objects (e.g., ropes, chairs, Frisbees, cones, pieces of carpet) into a defined area. Pair up the participants (or if you're working with an odd number, have a group of three). Blindfold one of the pair. The task of the other person in the pair is to verbally guide his or her partner to the other side of the minefield without allowing him or her to touch any object or anybody else. The sighted person is not allowed into the minefield but must verbally guide the partner from the side. If a touch is made, no matter how slight, the person takes off the blindfold and returns to the beginning to start again. Participants can begin at any point around the edge of the minefield but must successfully traverse to the opposite side of the field. Naturally, because the entire group is doing the task at the same time, the noise level is considerable. Participation in Minefield can lead to discussion of issues such as empathy, communication (terminology, speaking the same language, clarity of instructions), and support.

How Many Participants?

Four or more.

What Type of Equipment?

⊚ A range of objects. Almost anything will work—balls, boxes, Frisbees, hoops, chairs, ropes, trash cans, cones, or any combination of these.

⊚ A rope or other boundary markers to indicate the perimeter of the minefield.

Where?

Any defined area. The more people involved, the larger the space should be. As a guide, an area that is 10 square feet is ideal for a group of four minefield explorers.

Safety Considerations

Avoid using objects that may be sharp or might otherwise provoke injury.

Helpful Hints

⊚ Placing more objects on the floor or creating additional height (e.g., ropes suspended at knee height between two boxes) increases the degree of difficulty.

⑥ Larger groups can break into teams rather than pairs. If using teams, either one person can try to guide all the others through the minefield, or a group of people can try to guide a single individual.

Extensions and Variations

⑥ Within the minefield have a number of help objects, such as Ping-Pong balls or small (silver dollar-size) pieces of carpet. Guides verbally lead their person to a help object and instruct them in how to pick it up without touching anything else in the minefield. Help objects are equivalent to a "get out of jail free" card. If the person has a help object and then touches something, he or she drops the help object and is permitted to continue the course. This variation can lead to discussions about what support systems we have in our lives.

⑥ Have a unique object within the minefield that if successfully retrieved within a specified time keeps the minefield from exploding. All blindfolded participants usually strive to retrieve this object, which then brings safety to everyone. Introduce a discussion about how opponents can work together for the common good.

⑥ Have safe objects (objects that do not "explode" the minefield) within the minefield that are worth points. Each minefield explorer tries to collect as many points as possible within a specified period of time.

6.11   GROUP PUSH-UP

18+

The Basics

Group Push-Up is not for novices! It requires considerable upper body strength and effective communication. Success is not guaranteed! Issue a challenge to the group: "How many of the group can you combine to do a group push-up?" The first person assumes a normal push-up position, except that his or her feet or shins rest on the next person's shoulders. A long, straight line of connected push-ups is the goal (rarely achieved). This can be an enjoyable activity, but the facilitator needs to be very careful that one or two individuals do not get blamed for the lack of success of the entire group. The group task is to accommodate the strengths and limitations of all its members.

The Group Push-Up is a demanding activity. Be sure to start with small groups of two or three before trying to make the group larger.

How Many Participants?
Three or more.

What Type of Equipment?
No equipment needed!

Where?
Indoors or outdoors.

Safety Considerations
The facilitator needs to be aware of how fatiguing this activity is to the muscles. Even if the group has not achieved success, move on to the next activity after a specified length of time. You can always return to the challenge another day!

Helpful Hints
- An effective strategy is to begin with small groups (e.g., groups of two or three) and then gradually make the groups larger.
- Encourage the group to communicate so that all participants begin and end the push-up at the same time.

Extensions and Variations
- Form a circle. No one has their feet on the ground.
- Particularly strong athletes can be further challenged by adding a clap at the top of the push-up. This variation is best left to groups of two or three.

6.12   USE IT OR LOSE IT

13+

The Basics

Team communication and cooperation are imperative for success, particularly in interactive sports. Use It or Lose It is a difficult and potentially frustrating team challenge. Remember that the activities in this chapter are sequenced from easy to more difficult, the latter requiring greater cooperation, communication, and trust.

Find two lines on the floor approximately 30 feet apart (the width of a volleyball court). Provide the team with blocks (ideally, four blocks for every seven people). The blocks serve as stepping stones. The objective is to move the team from one line to the other without touching the ground between the two lines. The blocks must always be held or have downward pressure on them. Failure to abide by this rule results in the immediate removal of the block (as if it has been swept away in a river with a fast-flowing current). If anyone steps on the ground, the entire team moves back to the beginning. All team members need to remain linked through physical contact at all times. Failure to do so means all members move back to the beginning.

The frustration that Use It or Lose It often generates can be useful as it raises a range of discussion points (e.g., leadership skills, group organization, and perseverance).

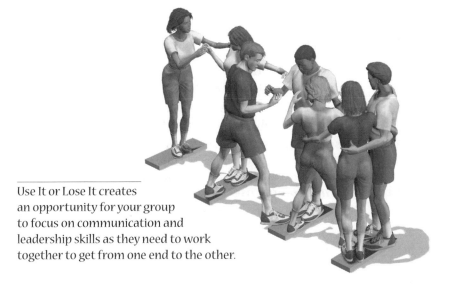

Use It or Lose It creates
an opportunity for your group
to focus on communication and
leadership skills as they need to work
together to get from one end to the other.

How Many Participants?

Six to 15 people on each team; you can have one or more teams.

What Type of Equipment?

⊚ Wooden blocks, roughly 12" × 8" × 3". If you are working at a school, get the shop class to make them for you.

⊚ Ropes or lines about 30 feet apart. Existing lines on a volleyball court work well. Ropes can be used as lines. The length of the ropes will depend on the number of groups (roughly 8 feet per group).

Where?

⊚ Indoors or outdoors.

⊚ An area approximately 40' × 10' if there is only one group; 40' × 40' if there are two to four groups.

Safety Considerations

Check blocks for rough edges that could cause splinters.

Helpful Hints

⊚ Failure can be potentially beneficial to the group to show that no team succeeds all of the time.

⊚ Plan time for discussion after the activity; consider topics such as leadership, communication, and dealing with frustration.

⊚ Don't be a softie—this is supposed to be challenging. If a block is abandoned for even a split second, seize it!

⊚ To add to the atmosphere, create a scenario—for example, the participants live on the planet Xergon and in 15 minutes it will explode. To save their race they must evacuate to planet Zifed using these life-support systems.

Extensions and Variations

⊚ Place a time limit (e.g., 10 minutes) on the group.

⊚ Blindfold some members of the team. This variation shows how individuals who are visually impaired can be included in this activity.

⊚ Designate some members as having certain disabilities (e.g., a broken leg or arm, inability to speak). This variation demonstrates how ambulatory individuals with disabilities (e.g., amputees) can be included in Use It or Lose It.

⊚ No speaking is allowed from any team member once he or she has started.

⊚ Each team member carries an object (e.g., eggs, balloons).

One-on-One Competitions

The idea of one-on-one competitions is fairly self-explanatory. Ideally, all of the activities in this chapter are used with a variety of people, rather than pairs that always stick together. With groups it is easy enough to have people change partners at a particular signal (e.g., a whistle). The idea is not to keep a record of results to see who "wins." Instead, participants have an opportunity to challenge themselves while interacting with different people, but the format is always one-on-one.

One-on-one competitions can be used as quick activities to fill in the gaps between more sport-specific drills or as part of a warm-up.

7.1   TOE TAPPER

8+

The Basics

Toe Tapper requires participants to be light on their feet. They need considerable concentration to be successful. Partners face each other and place their hands on the shoulders of their partner. Arms are straight. The objective is to try to step on the toes of the other person.

How Many Participants?

One or more pairs.

What Type of Equipment?

No equipment needed!

The basic version of Toe Tapper (left) requires only two participants, while the "free-for-all" variation (right) gives more people the opportunity to play.

Where?

Any nonslip surface.

Safety Considerations

- Because this is a quick-moving game, participants have virtually no opportunity to lift their legs high enough to cause damage when they come down.
- Participants must avoid wearing cleats, golf shoes, or steel-toed boots. Either everyone should be barefoot or everyone should wear tennis shoes.

Helpful Hints

- Remind people that it is useful to stay on the balls of the feet to be able to make quick movements to avoid the opponent.
- Toe Tapper can be fatiguing, both physically and mentally. Keep the bouts short.

Extensions and Variations

- Instead of participants staying in pairs, have groups of five or more form a circle holding hands. The objective is to tap the toes of a neighbor.
- If you change the rules and do not stipulate that hands must be placed on the opponent's shoulders, participants can use more space and possibly use different strategies.
- Alternatively, have a free-for-all in a small area where anyone can tap anyone else's toes.

7.2   KNEE TAG

8+

The Basics

Knee Tag is a great energizer that can be used as a break during classroom sessions or somewhat monotonous drills. Partners begin this activity facing each other. The object is to try to tag the other person behind the knee with an open hand. No head butting allowed! Both people must be standing for a tag to count (that is, no tackling the person to the ground and then tagging him or her behind the knee). Someone going in for a touch must completely disengage before touching again (no multiple touches allowed).

How Many Participants?
One or more pairs.

What Type of Equipment?
No equipment needed!

Where?
Any nonslip surface.

Safety Considerations
- With some groups, you may need to indicate that a participant is not allowed to hold the other person's hands or arms to avoid or make a tag. The only form of defense is to move out of the way.
- Anyone who finds it difficult or painful to shuffle sideways with bent knees should avoid this activity.

Helpful Hints
Knee Tag can be played as a competition (e.g., the first player to make four touches wins), or for specified lengths of time.

Extensions and Variations
To dramatically increase difficulty, have participants hold a volleyball between their knees.

7.3   SOCK STEALING

18+

The Basics
Both partners remove their shoes but keep on their socks. They begin by sitting with legs crossed while facing each other about 3 or 4 feet apart. The goal is to try to remove one of the other person's socks while keeping on their own. Sock Stealing is a fun and frantic break from the norm. The person who first gets a sock off the other person wins.

How Many Participants?
One or more pairs.

What Type of Equipment?
Socks (preferably clean ones!).

Where?
Indoors (socks get too disgusting outdoors).

Safety Considerations
⑤ Stipulate that tackling, tickling, and slapping are not allowed.

⑤ A lot of body contact is involved in this activity. Have a predetermined signal that participants can use to indicate that they want to stop because they are in a particularly uncomfortable or potentially dangerous position. When the signal is given, play must stop immediately.

Helpful Hints
Use this activity toward the beginning of a session, before socks get to a point where the owner doesn't want to touch them, let alone someone else! Alternatively, provide a clean pair of socks for each person.

Extensions and Variations
⑤ Have the participants start by sitting back to back.

⑤ For athletes involved in contact sports, participants can begin Sock Stealing in a standing position. Use mats for this variation.

8+

7.4   TUG-TO-WIN

The Basics
Balance is a major component of Tug-to-Win in that the activity is a hopping tug-of-war. Partners face each other. Each person extends the left leg in the air toward the partner. Each person grasps the foot of the partner with the right hand. With the left hand they grasp the other person's remaining free hand. As the participants hop backward, the objective is to try to pull the other person across a line. If contact is broken in any way, the pair starts again.

How Many Participants?
One or more pairs.

What Type of Equipment?
Two lines or markers about 15 feet apart.

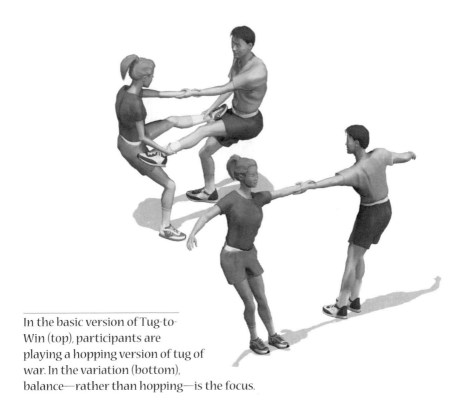

In the basic version of Tug-to-Win (top), participants are playing a hopping version of tug of war. In the variation (bottom), balance—rather than hopping—is the focus.

Where?
Any nonslip surface.

Safety Considerations
⑥ Be sure the playing area is free of obstacles.

⑥ The tugging can be achieved only through hopping, not by simply using upper body strength to pull the other person off balance. Demonstrating the correct and incorrect methods of tugging is the best way of communicating this rule to youngsters.

⑥ Be sure the participants are wearing shoes that have good traction (socks alone are lethal).

Helpful Hints
⑥ Participants will be less hesitant doing Tug-to-Win on grass than on a hard floor.

⑥ After a few minutes, switch legs.

⑥ To be equitable, try to match partners of similar size (height, leg length, weight).

Extensions and Variations

Partners grasp each other by the wrist (left hands). Then, side by side but facing in opposite directions, each person tries to pull the opponent over a line. Both feet are used for balance, so no hopping is required. Be sure to remove wristwatches for this one.

7.5   LEG WRESTLING

8+

The Basics

Leg Wrestling probably won't make it to ESPN as arm wrestling has, but it challenges both flexibility and strength throughout the entire body. Partners lie down side by side on their backs, with heads pointing in opposite directions. The waist of one person should be in line with the waist of the partner. Each person then raises the inside leg, bends the knee, and locks legs with the partner. By pulling their locked legs down toward the ground, participants try to flip their partner or turn them sideways (i.e., break position). Hands should remain palms down at the sides at all times.

Leg Wrestling develops flexibility and strength, and can be used indoors or outdoors.

How Many Participants?
One or more pairs.

What Type of Equipment?
Everyone should wear shorts or sweats.

Where?
Any clean floor or grassy area.

Safety Considerations
People with neck or back trouble should avoid this activity.

Helpful Hints
⊚ Once again, matching people in terms of size intensifies the competition.

⊚ Participants should avoid wearing tight shorts.

Extensions and Variations
To take out the component of upper body strength, have participants fold hands on the stomach instead of placing them on the ground. When playing this game outdoors, some people try to gain leverage by grabbing clumps of grass; this is not only cheating, but can be bad for the lawn.

7.6   THUMB WRESTLING

8+

The Basics
Thumb Wrestling is not particularly demanding physically, but it is an activity that can be used during a break or as a method of allocating teams. Sporting prowess is not a guarantee of success in that anyone with a functioning hand can become a thumb wrestling guru; therefore many individuals with disabilities can participate successfully in thumb wrestling. Partners face each other and move as if to shake hands but place their fingers against the opponent's fingers. Both people then curl their fingers until their knuckles are against the opponent's palm. The thumbs remain on top. The goal is to try to pin the opponent's thumb with one's own. The wrestling begins with a count of three. On the count of '1,' thumbs move to the left, on the count of '2,' thumbs move to the right. On the count of '3,' thumbs move to the left. As soon as thumbs

have made contact with the hands on the third count, the wrestling begins! Elbows must remain next to the body (no high elbows allowed).

How Many Participants?
One or more pairs.

What Type of Equipment?
No equipment needed!

Where?
Anywhere!

Safety Considerations
Long fingernails can be problematic. Perhaps pair those with long fingernails together so they can mutually agree to have a slightly looser grip.

Helpful Hints
Thumb Wrestling can be a fun way of deciding who goes first in the next activity or splitting a group in half (winners in one group, runners-up in the other).

Extensions and Variations
⑥ Participants thumb wrestle while treading water. Keep the hands above water at all times!

⑥ Participants thumb wrestle while blindfolded. The unsighted version often requires greater concentration and may help develop kinesthetic awareness.

⑥ Have two pairs join together to form a square, with each person facing his or her original partner. One pair crosses their arms; the other pair holds their hands out without crossing. Grasp the nearest hand. Everyone should be holding the hands of two different people, but always right hand to right hand and left hand to left hand. On the count of three, everyone wrestles. It is challenging to keep track of two competitions at the same time.

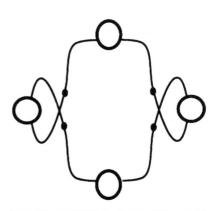

In this variation of Thumb Wrestling, each person is wrestling two people at the same time.

7.7 LOCK 'N' PULL

8+

The Basics
Partners sit back to back with legs bent and feet together. Throughout the activity the feet must stay together and in the midline of the body. Partners interlock their arms. On a signal each person pulls to their right, trying to bring their opponent's shoulder down to the ground. If partners are evenly matched, Lock 'n' Pull provides considerable strength training through isometric contractions.

How Many Participants?
One or more pairs.

What Type of Equipment?
No equipment needed!

Where?
Any clean, nonslip surface.

Safety Considerations
When sitting back to back, people need to be as close together as possible, with no space between bodies.

Helpful Hints
⊚ Try to match individuals in terms of weight and height.

⊚ Careful monitoring of feet is imperative. Moving a leg out to the side is definitely cheating!

Extensions and Variations
On a predetermined signal (e.g., calling "change"), everyone changes the direction they are pulling. This can sometimes give someone who is consistently losing an opportunity to be successful.

7.8 FAKE AND PUSH

8+

The Basics

Everyone faces their partner, with 2 to 3 feet between them. Each person must stand with feet together. The feet are not allowed to move at any time. With fingers pointed up, partners place their palms against each other's. The objective is to make the partner lose his or her balance by either pushing, dodging, or feinting. Once the game starts the palms do not need to stay together; people can temporarily move their hands out of the way. So if one person is giving a big push, the partner's moving the hands out of the way may result in the pusher's momentum carrying him or her off balance. In Fake and Push, the simple movement of a hand can turn an almost certain loss into victory. Moving a foot signifies loss of balance; participants don't actually continue until someone falls down.

In Fake and Push, the objective is to make your opponent lose balance without moving your own feet.

How Many Participants?

One or more pairs.

What Type of Equipment?

No equipment needed!

Where?

Any level surface.

Safety Considerations

Players must not make contact with any part of the partner's body other than the palms. In other words, a person cannot maintain balance by leaning on the partner.

Helpful Hints

⑥ If both players lose their balance at the same time, play begins again.

⑥ If both players have short arms, they should stand fairly close together. Partners with long arms should stand further apart. When arm length is uneven, split the difference.

Extensions and Variations

⑥ Palms stay in contact at all times, but no sudden movements are allowed. This version has the feel of a tai chi exercise. It is probably too difficult for most children.

⑥ Before starting play, each person turns around three times on the spot.

⑥ Players begin with left hand to left hand and right hand to right hand. This starting stance creates the added dimension of whether or not one's arms are crossed. Only one of the two people will have their arms crossed at any point during the competition. Generally it is more difficult to maintain one's balance and push when one's arms are crossed.

7.9   BLOW IT

8+

The Basics

When you need a hilarious, zany activity, nothing fits the bill better than Blow It. Relying on lung function more than anything else, this activity is guaranteed to keep both participants and spectators laughing. Place a Ping-Pong ball on the ground between two opponents. On a given signal each player tries to blow the ball past the opponent until it crosses a preestablished line or marker. Players are allowed to move.

How Many Participants?

One or more pairs.

What Type of Equipment?

⑥ One Ping-Pong ball for each pair.

⑥ Lines or markers.

Where?

Any clean area. Half a volleyball court is enough space for about six pairs.

Safety Considerations

⑥ If players are competing on grass, check the area for hidden thorns, sticks, or other potentially dangerous items.

⑥ Because people can get light-headed from doing this activity, you may need to establish time limits. Begin with a limit of 30 seconds. Extend the time limit as players become more experienced.

⑥ Either assign same-sex partners or ensure that females are wearing appropriate (higher-necked) shirts.

Helpful Hints

⑥ The success of short, strong blows versus long, steady blows will depend on the tactics of each opponent. Trial and error is the only way to determine what works best!

⑥ Adjusting the width of the playing field will influence tactics. If the goal line is relatively close, one unblocked blow could win the game. If the ball has to cover more distance, players will need a different approach.

Extensions and Variations

   ◉ Matches will move quickly on a gym floor. For a real challenge, try it on grass.

   ◉ Try Blow It using straws.

   ◉ Try two balls at once—an individual has to have both balls cross the line for a win.

Fitness Activities

Basic fitness training can get boring. Instead of doing repetitive push-ups or pull-ups or running just to run, use these general fitness activities to avoid hearing your athletes or students groan, "Oh no, not again." The activities presented in this chapter can develop both cardiovascular fitness and muscular strength. An advantage of these games over standard fitness activities is that the majority of them contain a cooperative component. Read on for unique activities with an ulterior motive.

8.1   PAIR PULL-UPS

13+

● ●

The Basics

Chin-ups can get boring, and they may be impossible for some people. Pair Pull-Ups work on upper body strength, but the challenge and enjoyment often keep people from noticing that aspect of the activity.

Participants are grouped in pairs. One person lies on his or her back. The partner stands facing the person with one foot on either side of the partner's chest. Partners grasp hands. The person standing pulls up the partner. The person being pulled up must maintain a completely stiff body so that only the heels touch the ground.

How Many Participants?

One or more pairs.

What Type of Equipment?

No equipment needed!

Where?

Flat, clean ground or floor.

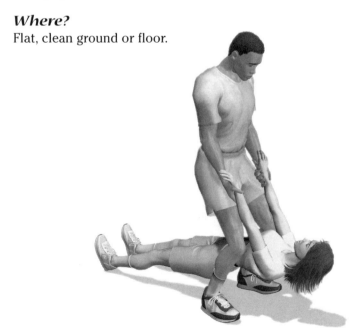

Pair Pull-Ups emphasizes upper body strength, and it requires no equipment.

Safety Considerations

◎ It is important that pairs communicate with each other regarding their readiness as well as possible fatigue.

◎ The person standing may need to bend at the knees to help keep a straight back.

Helpful Hints

If participants have been competing against each other (e.g., some of the one-on-one competitions from chapter 7), the leader may need to remind them that cooperation is required for Pair Pull-Ups.

Extensions and Variations

◎ As a variation, the person on the bottom can do pull-ups. The standing person's feet need to be near the partner's armpits so the shoulders are aligned above the other person's shoulders. The person who is upright must stand up straight with shoulders back and head up, providing stability for the person on the ground doing pull-ups.

◎ A more dynamic version of Pair Pull-Ups requires two people to sit facing each other with knees bent and feet together. Grasping each other's hands (or wrists), both partners try to create a seesaw effect. One person stands as the other lies down, and then vice versa. The challenge is to make the transition as smooth as possible.

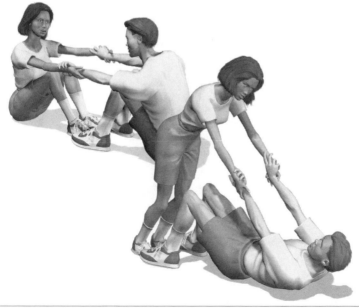

In this variation of Pair Pull-Ups, participants attempt to create a seesaw effect.

8.2   KEEP IT UP

8+

The Basics

To add some party atmosphere to your class or practice session, throw in a game of Keep It Up as part of the warm-up. Each person begins with two balloons. On cue, everyone hits their balloons high into the air. The goal is for the group to keep all of the balloons in the air by hitting them with their hands. Anyone able to visually track a balloon can participate in this game; therefore participants in wheelchairs or those with other physical disabilities can easily be included.

How Many Participants?

Three or more.

What Type of Equipment?

At least two balloons for each person.

In Keep It Up, the goal is for the group to keep all the balloons up in the air.

Where?
Indoors, unless you have a day with absolutely no wind.

Safety Considerations
In between bouts, give the participants a chance to relax their necks by having them tuck their chins.

Helpful Hints
⑥ Get the participants to blow up the balloons for you.

⑥ If the group finds the activity too easy, the leader can add more balloons.

⑥ It may be worth investing in good-quality balloons, because cheap ones tend to pop without much provocation. If cheap balloons are the only ones available, be sure to have extras (already blown up) in reserve.

Extensions and Variations
⑥ Designate pairs and assign each pair a number. Have one pair with a total of four balloons in the middle of a defined circle (e.g., as found on a basketball court). Everyone else is scattered around the circle. The initial pair begins by hitting their balloons in the air. When the leader calls out a number, the initial pair leaves the circle and the pair with the corresponding number enters the circle. The balloons must stay off the floor and in the circle at all times.

⑥ Two teams separated by a net (preferably a volleyball net; a badminton net would be too low) try to keep the balloons from hitting the floor on their side of the net while trying to get them to fall on the other side. Balloons are not allowed to pass under or around the net.

⑥ Soccer players may benefit from playing Keep It Up with the restriction that they use only heads, knees or feet to contact balloons.

8.3   PUSH TO STAND

8+

The Basics
Although the basic Push to Stand is just that—basic—the variations can provide challenges to suit almost anyone. Begin with two people who sit back to back with legs bent and feet together. Partners link arms. The pair then push against each other to reach a standing position.

How Many Participants?
Two or more.

What Type of Equipment?
No equipment needed!

Where?
Any clean, flat surface.

Safety Considerations
To avoid the possibility of wrenching their shoulders, partners need to coordinate the start so that they begin pushing at the same time.

Helpful Hints
The trick for Push to Stand is to have equal pressure pushing on the backs. Partners can accommodate height or weight differences by applying different amounts of pressure. For example, participants need to push harder against heavier partners or apply pressure with only part of their back against shorter partners.

Extensions and Variations
⑥ Have pairs try to stand without linking arms. The focus should be on upper body and abdominal stability rather than just pushing with the legs. You may want to try this one on mats.

⑥ Challenge elite athletes to stand using only one leg. This variation is appropriate only for older participants (i.e., at least 16) and those who are fit.

⑥ Once two people successfully stand (with linked arms and using two legs), try it with three people, then four. See how many people can successfully stand as one.

8.4   FANTASY WRITING

8+

The Basics
Fantasy Writing may seem childish, but with the proper introduction and enthusiasm from the leader it can be an enjoyable method of working on shoulder strength. All individuals stand holding their implement (e.g., hockey stick, tennis racket) at the very end of the grip. With the

arm and implement extended, each person uses the implement to write in the air. In pairs or small groups, participants take turns writing their names in the air until everyone knows everyone else's name. Once names have been learned, Fantasy Writing can be used to have individuals guess the words or pictures that others draw.

How Many Participants?
Two or more.

What Type of Equipment?
One implement for each person. Possible implements include hockey (field or ice) or lacrosse sticks and tennis, squash, or badminton rackets.

Where?
Anywhere!

Safety Considerations
With people waving sticks in the air, be sure there is adequate space between participants.

Helpful Hints
- Individuals with either weak upper body strength or heavy implements (e.g., baseball bats) can choke up on the implement to write. The closer to the end the implement is held, the greater the shoulder strength required to perform the activity.
- Keeping the covers on rackets makes them heavier.

Extensions and Variations
- For an added mental challenge, have participants write the alphabet (or specific words) backward.
- Instead of individuals drawing, have everyone stand in a circle. Each participant has an implement and holds it out straight with one arm. Instead of holding the end of the implement as in the basic Fantasy Writing, individuals hold the middle, so that the implement points up and down. On cue, everyone passes their implement to the right or left by tossing it lightly into the air in front of them (everyone must pass in the same direction). This is more difficult than it might sound, because everyone has to turn to catch the implement being passed to them from their neighbor as soon as they have released theirs. If passing the implements to the right, participants use their right hands. When passing to the left, they use their left hands. For the longevity of equipment, perform this version on grass. Challenge participants to see how many group passes and catches they can make successfully (and successively) in 30 seconds.

8.5   DRY SURFING

8+

The Basics

Dry Surfing works on leg strength and balance without the need for getting wet or living near a beach. Place a crash mat (a mat between six and 12 inches thick) on top of a bunch of basketballs. Have at least one person stand at each side of the mat. One person stands on top of the mat. The aim is for that person to remain standing. The others gently move the mat over the balls. The only downside of this activity is that not everyone can "surf" at the same time.

How Many Participants?

Five or more.

Dry Surfing is a fun way for participants to work on balance and leg strength without living near a beach.

What Type of Equipment?

⑥ Twelve or more basketballs.

⑥ One crash mat (roughly 8' × 5').

Where?

Indoors (gym).

Safety Considerations

Dry Surfing is challenging. The mat movers do not need to be vigorous for the surfer to lose balance. Start with the person just standing, then slowly introduce movement into the activity. Be sure that the mat is in an open space (no walls nearby).

Helpful Hints

Mat movers may find it easier to crouch and just gently push the mat in a give-and-take action.

Extensions and Variations

Surfers with brilliant balance can increase the challenge of the activity by closing their eyes.

8.6   IMAGINARY SKIPPING

8+

The Basics

Skipping rope provides great cardiovascular benefits, but only if people can keep jumping. To avoid the time delays involved with twisted ropes or tripping athletes, try Imaginary Skipping. The leader brings around an imaginary bag from which each person selects an imaginary rope. Participants are challenged to skip in a variety of ways—for example, skipping forward, skipping backward, doing double jumps, crossing the rope, or turning around.

How Many Participants?

One or more.

What Type of Equipment?

No equipment needed!

Where?
Any flat ground.

Safety Considerations
Remind participants about the importance of bending their knees every time they land.

Helpful Hints
The leader's enthusiasm and belief in Imaginary Skipping makes or breaks this activity. Individuals who may not be able to jump rope because of coordination difficulties or mild physical disabilities can enthusiastically take part in Imaginary Skipping. With an energetic leader, this activity can be successful with any age group.

Extensions and Variations
- Have participants pair up, with one person turning the "rope" and the other jumping with him or her.
- Have participants use a larger "rope," with two people turning and multiple people jumping in the middle.

8.7   BASKET CASE

8+

The Basics
Although often part of standard drills in sports such as volleyball, Basket Case can be a fun way of keeping up the heart rate. If the basic version seems too mundane, try the variation! Place a basket in the center of the floor. Disperse balls around the gym. The goal of the participants is to fill the basket. The leader stands at the basket and empties it as fast as possible, one ball at a time.

How Many Participants?
Four or more.

What Type of Equipment?
- One basket (or bucket, plastic trash can, or ball trolley).
- Balls (approximately three for every two people).

Where?
A gym or tennis court.

Safety Considerations
Emptiers should either roll the balls or throw them underhand. The balls should never be higher than waist height.

Helpful Hints
⑥ If there are only a small number of participants or the participants are not particularly in shape, use fewer balls, restrict the size of the area, or help participants out by throwing the balls in their general direction.

⑥ To avoid congestion with a large number of participants, provide more than one basket.

Extensions and Variations
Have two teams. One team tries to keep the basket full while the other tries to keep it empty. Members of the emptying team are allowed to take out only one ball at a time (and can fling it below waist height anywhere in the gym). Before taking out another ball, the emptier must run and touch a designated line or wall. The game begins with half the balls in the basket and half scattered around the gym.

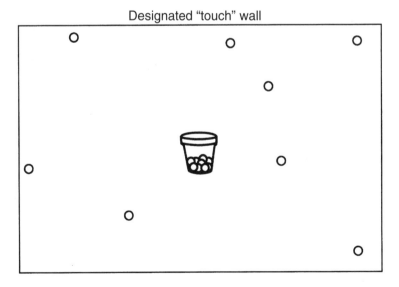

In this variation of Basket Case, the people emptying the basket have to run and touch the "touch" wall after removing each ball.

Relays and Races

This chapter contains a rabble-rousing range of recommended relays. Mention the word relay, and 99.9% of people understand the basic concept. Few of us have outgrown our competitive urges (and some of us may even have strengthened them as we have gotten older).

When presented with a relay, we tend to put in 100%. Although the specific benefits of the relays and races in this chapter vary, all of them create enthusiasm.

9.1   TUNNEL BALL PLUS

13+

The Basics

Basic tunnel ball is a popular school activity in some countries. Each team stands in a line, one person behind the other with feet apart. The person at the head of the line holds a ball, which is then passed between the legs from person to person through the line. The last person in line collects the ball and runs to the front. This continues until the original leader is once again at the head of the line.

Tunnel Ball Plus requires that everyone line up side by side. Everyone except for the first and last person in line assumes the push-up position. The person in front rolls the ball (as in 10-pin bowling) under the line of participants and then forms the push-up position. The last person in line collects the ball, runs to the front, rolls the ball through the line, and then forms the push-up position. The new last person in line stands up ready to collect the ball. This continues until the original person is again first. People may need to temporarily balance on one arm if the ball slows down or gets off track.

How Many Participants?

Groups of six or more.

Tunnel Ball Plus requires participants to line up in push-up position as the ball is rolled under their bodies.

What Type of Equipment?
One ball for each group.

Where?
Any flat, clean ground.

Safety Considerations
When in the push-up position, participants need to keep their bodies straight and their backsides down. If they cannot maintain the push-up position, then try one of the variations.

Helpful Hints
The closer together people are in the line, the quicker the ball can be passed (because it has less distance to travel). If you want to increase the amount of muscle stamina required, space the participants farther apart.

Extensions and Variations
- Instead of the push-up position, participants assume the V-sit position (legs and back straight). The ball is then passed across laps until the last person receives it.
- Have a different-colored ball for each team (any number of teams is possible as long as there are more than one). Yell "scatter" and then throw the balls around the gym or field. Each team must then run to their ball, line up, and then complete the tunnel ball activity.

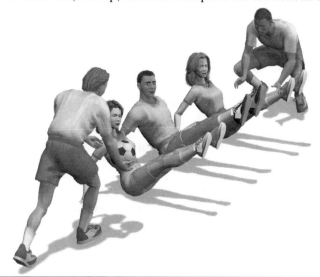

In this V-sit variation of Tunnel Ball, the ball is passed across the laps of the participants.

9.2   OVER-UNDER

8+

The Basics

In basic over-under relays, members of a team line up one behind the other. A ball is passed over the head of the first person and then between the legs of the second. When the last person in line gets the ball, he or she runs to the front and begins the process again. In our version of Over-Under, the participants stand at least an arm's length behind the person in front of them with their feet as far apart as possible. They then pass the ball using the same over-under technique. If the ball touches the ground, it must be returned to the front and passed again.

How Many Participants?

Teams of seven or more.

What Type of Equipment?

One ball for each team.

Where?

Any flat ground.

Safety Considerations

⑥ Try to place the really flexible people next to the really inflexible ones. When people with limited range of motion are placed next to each other, they may tend to strain something in their desire to succeed.

⑥ Be sure participants have warmed up before beginning this activity.

Helpful Hints

The greater the distance between people, the more stretching they will have to do to pass the ball between them.

Extensions and Variations

⑥ To make the muscles work a bit, use a medicine ball or a jelly ball.

⑥ Using a ball about the size of a volleyball, allow participants to use only one hand.

⑥ For a real challenge, blindfold the participants. Not only does this require greater communication as the ball is passed down the line, but the person moving to the front of the line needs to be guided verbally.

9.3   DIZZY RELAY

13+

The Basics
Lay one stick or pole for each team on the ground about 50 feet from the starting line. The teams line up behind the starting line. The first participant in each line runs to the pole and places one end of it on or in the ground. With both hands on the other end of the pole, he or she then places the forehead on the hands and then runs around the pole six times. After the sixth complete turn, the participant places the pole on the ground and returns to the starting line to tag the next person. Although skaters who are used to spinning may find this activity easy, most people will have a hard time running a straight line!

How Many Participants?
Two teams of five or more.

What Type of Equipment?
⑤ One stick or pole for each team (baseball bats work).

⑤ A starting line.

Where?
Sand or very soft grass.

Safety Considerations
Space the teams further apart from each other than you would in a normal running relay. Even with the extra space, people don't always end up returning to their own teams. To decrease the potential for collisions, limit the number of teams to two.

Helpful Hints
⑤ As people get dizzy, they tend to place more and more weight on the pole. Be sure the implements you use can support the weight!

⑤ Require the team to chant the name of the person running back. This gives the dizzy runner an auditory cue and encourages name memorization.

⑤ The leader may want to stand at the end by the poles to ensure that everyone completes the required number of revolutions.

Extensions and Variations
For a real comedy of errors, have the participants skip or hop instead of run.

9.4   TEAM JUMP

The Basics

Teams begin at a starting line. One person from each team does a standing broad jump. Their performance is marked by the part of the body that lands closest to the start (i.e., if they fall backward, the point of reference might be a hand or one's backside; otherwise it would be the heel). The next person on each team uses that reference as their starting point. Team Jump is not a race but rather a challenge to cover the most distance with the same number of people. Team Jump encourages people to try their hardest regardless of their ability, because every inch counts.

How Many Participants?

Teams of three or more.

What Type of Equipment?

⑥ A starting line.

⑥ Something to mark the progressive starting points (chalk, a stick—virtually anything).

Where?

Any flat area.

Safety Considerations

Because maximum efforts are involved, be sure that all participants warm up and stretch before beginning the activity.

Helpful Hints

You can require jumpers to do two jumps in a row or have more than one turn at jumping. Try to make teams even in terms of ability.

Extensions and Variations

⑥ Rather than seeing how far a team can get with a specified number of people or jumps, see how many jumps it takes to cover a particular distance.

⑥ For a real thigh workout, do Team Jump in deep sand.

⑥ Blindfold the people who are jumping; doing so makes it harder for them to maintain their balance when they land.

8+

9.5   PROGRESSIVE RELAY

The Basics

For sports or activities that require running as either a warm-up or a necessary component of training, merely running around a track or a field can get boring. Progressive Relay combines running with teamwork and group competition. All participants in Progressive Relay run the same distance. Create a set course, either to an object and back or around something. The first person from each team runs the course, returns to the start, and then grabs the hand of the next person on their team. The two run the course together. This continues until the entire team is running the course together, holding hands. After the circuit with the entire team, the person who began the race is released from the group at the start. The group is gradually depleted, in reverse order, until the last person to join the group runs the circuit alone.

How Many Participants?

Teams of four or more.

What Type of Equipment?

Course markers.

Where?

Almost anywhere.

Safety Considerations

If the course is outdoors and on uneven terrain, participants need to watch out for any obstacles or rough ground that might slow down any member of the running group.

Helpful Hints

You may need to remind speed demons that the pace has to be suitable for all participants who are running.

Extensions and Variations

Have two lines marked about 30 feet apart. The goal is to get the entire team from the first line to the second. The challenge is that no one can have their feet cross the second line unless they have been carried from the first line by teammates. The team begins by carrying one person from the first line to the second, being careful that the person being carried never touches the ground in between the two lines, and that the people doing the carrying don't cross the second line. Only those who have been carried across are able to cross the second line. Once someone has been carried across the line, that person can run back and help carry others across. To keep track of who has been carried across the line (and can therefore cross the second line any time they want), participants can be required to pick up a tennis ball the first time they cross the line. They must hold the tennis ball at all times—no passing it to other people. This extension of Progressive Relay is appropriate for ages 13 and older.

9.6   COLLECTIVE TALLY

8+

The Basics
Commonly referred to as Rob the Nest in some countries, Collective Tally can be organized as a relay or as an ongoing game. Place a bucket in each corner of the gym or playing area. In the center of the area have a collection of balls. Divide the group into four teams and assign each team to a different corner. Players line up behind their bucket, facing the center. Every member of each team is given a number, in sequence. Player 1 in each team runs to the center, collects a ball, places it in the team bucket, and then tags player 2. This continues until either everyone in one team has had a turn or a team has managed to collect four balls. The objective is to fill up your team's bucket before the other teams fill up theirs. Each participant has the choice of collecting a ball from the middle or stealing a ball from another bucket.

How Many Participants?
Four teams of three or more.

What Type of Equipment?
- ◉ Twelve balls or other small objects. Tennis balls, baseballs or softballs work well.
- ◉ Four buckets or other containers.

Where?
A flat defined area.

In Collective Tally, each team tries to fill up its bucket before the other teams fill theirs.

Safety Considerations
If not forewarned, players who are awaiting their turn tend to collect around the bucket and prevent outsiders from stealing. Collective Tally is a noncontact activity. Players need free access at all times; therefore, no goalkeeping is allowed.

Helpful Hints
⑥ To make it easier to see the number of balls a given team has collected, place the balls inside a hoop instead of in a bucket.

⑥ If small balls are used, be alert to crafty individuals who try to collect more than one at a time.

Extensions and Variations
⑥ Place a time limit on the game. All teams continue playing until the end of the stipulated period. The team with the most balls at the end of the period wins.

⑥ The leader calls out one or more numbers. People collect a ball only when their number is called. If the ball has not been deposited in the team bucket before the leader calls out the next number(s), the ball must be dropped. Allow players to continue to collect balls (still one at a time) until the next number is called.

⑥ Require participants to dribble the ball.

9.7 MISSING SOMETHING

8+

The Basics

Pairs race against each other over a specified distance. The hitch is that one person in each pair is blindfolded and the other can have only one foot in contact with the ground. Pairs can develop their own strategies as to how they want to organize themselves. If the fourth foot touches the ground, the pair must return to the start. Missing Something requires people to depend on their partners as well as help them. This activity also allows people to be creative with their strategies.

How Many Participants?

Two or more pairs.

What Type of Equipment?

- One blindfold for each pair.
- Markers for the start and finish of the race.

Where?

Any flat defined area.

Safety Considerations

Giving participants time to try out their strategies increases the chances of the pairs remaining upright once the race begins.

Helpful Hints

- Be sure that everyone has an opportunity to be blindfolded.
- Individuals who are visually impaired or who have mild cerebral palsy can easily be integrated into this game.

Extensions and Variations

- Instead of pairs, have individuals work in threes. One person is still blindfolded, and the other two are tied together at the ankle (as in a three-legged race).
- Set up the activity as a relay with multiple pairs (or threes) on each team.

9.8   LEADING LINES

8+

The Basics

Leading Lines is effective in helping people improve their ability to change direction quickly. The competitive element often generates enthusiasm that would not be present in a standard drill. Participants form lines of approximately four people each, with the lines parallel to the front of the room or space. The people in each line stand side by side and hold hands. All lines begin in the center of the designated space, facing the leader. The leader calls out "left" or "right." Each line moves together as a group in the designated direction. The objective is for the person on either end of the line to touch a wall or sideline. The leader can either face the group and control the length of the activity by changing the direction before anyone reaches the sideline or wall, or face away from the group and randomly call directions.

In Leading Lines, each line moves together as a group in the direction designated by the leader.

How Many Participants?
Two or more lines of four or more.

What Type of Equipment?
Sidelines.

Where?
Any flat area.

Safety Considerations
If one member of a line is a bit slower than the others, the line might tend to drag or push that person.

Helpful Hints
If a line breaks (drops hands), the entire group must do 10 tuck jumps before relinking in the center.

Extensions and Variations
- Have each group line up one behind the other. All members of the group must touch the sideline or wall for the group to be successful.
- Include directions of "forward," "back," and "turn around."

9.9   OBSTACLE OPTIONS

8+

The Basics
Obstacle courses can work with any age group. The multitude of variations in Obstacle Options allows a leader to tailor the course to suit the group's fitness levels and training needs. Set up an obstacle course. To work on power, speed, or both, make the course relatively short but require people to jump over things, sprint short distances (possibly uphill), or perhaps throw or push objects quickly. Once the course has been completed, allow full recovery (i.e., at least 2 minutes) before participants repeat the course. To work on strength, design the course so that individuals must lift themselves or cover territory using techniques other than running or walking (e.g., crab walk). To emphasize cardiovascular endurance the obstacle course can be extremely varied, but

encourage people to be on the course for 15 to 20 minutes (or possibly to complete a 2-minute course 10 times but with less than 30 seconds of rest in between).

How Many Participants?
If racing, two or more.

What Type of Equipment?
⑥ Obstacles such as benches, tables, poles, nets, tires, ropes, and chin-up bars.

⑥ Course markers.

⑥ Stopwatch.

Where?
A large, obstacle-full area.

Safety Considerations
If any sections of the course require balance or progression above ground, you need to distribute mats for safety. Before a race begins, each participant should have the opportunity to walk through the course and become familiar with how to overcome the obstacles rather than having the first attempt be at full speed.

Helpful Hints
Encourage different groups to create challenging (but possible!) obstacle courses on different days (or different parts of a single session). Always be sure to check new courses for safety.

Extensions and Variations
Putting people in pairs or groups of three and having each person start the course when the previous person finishes provides a built-in recovery time. Each member of the group is to complete the course a specified number of times. This format sets up relay races between groups.

Games to Enhance Basic Sport Skills

The activities in this section facilitate the performance of basic sport skills. Rather than just repeating basic skills ad nauseam, individuals are able to practice them while confronting various challenges. These activities include either an element of competition, an added action to be performed simultaneously, or altered conditions under which the skill is performed. The aim of these general sport skill activities is to take the drudgery out of drills.

10.1   BEAT THE BALL

8+

The Basics
Many sports require speed and precision in passing. These sports often involve running as well. Beat the Ball encourages passers and catchers to work as quickly as possible while maintaining accuracy to try to be faster than a runner. Five or six people form a pattern as shown in the illustration on this page. The ball starts at one end and is passed from person to person until it reaches the other end; then it is passed from person to person back to the start. At the same time these players start passing the ball, a runner begins running around the entire group. The competition is to see who wins, the runner or the ball. After each race, everyone rotates a position to ensure a new runner as well as new end people in the throwing formation.

How Many Participants?
Six or more.

What Type of Equipment?
⑥ A ball.

⑥ Any equipment specific to the sport of the participants (e.g., mitts, field hockey sticks, or lacrosse sticks).

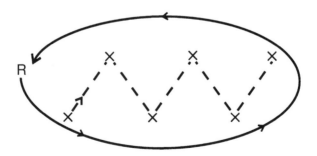

— → Path of ball   R Runner
—→ Path of runner   ✗ Throwers/catchers

After each Beat the Ball race, players rotate to allow everyone to be a runner and a thrower.

Where?

Indoors or outdoors.

Safety Considerations

If a hard ball is being thrown above waist height, the runner may want to run a predetermined distance in a location that is slightly away from the throwers rather than around them, just in case the throws are inaccurate.

Helpful Hints

Modifications will be needed in terms of distance or number of passers depending on the type of passing being done and the skill level of the participants. The aim is to make the running time and passing time as similar as possible. A useful guide is that eight passers take up a length of about 40 feet; hence the runner runs just over 80 feet.

Extensions and Variations

- Participants can use any type of pass in this activity: chest or bounce passes in basketball; sets or forearm passes in volleyball; pushes or hits in field hockey; or any other types of passes (e.g., soccer, lacrosse, netball, rugby).

- Beat the Ball can also take place in the pool with water polo; however, the swimmer should be allowed to swim in a straight line with a turn off a wall instead of having to swim in a circle around the passers. The passers may need to move the ball up and back through the formation twice to allow the swimmer enough time. Alternatively, make the swimming distance relatively short.

10.2   SHADOW

8+

The Basics

Shadow is an advanced form of follow the leader. While reacting to a leader, followers have to control a ball and be aware of everyone else in the area. Participants break into pairs, in which one person is designated as leader and the other as follower. Everyone has a ball. While dribbling, the leader tries to stay away from the follower. While dribbling, the follower tries to stay within arm's length of the leader. Because more than one pair is doing the activity at the same time, everyone has to be aware of traffic. Because of the emphasis on dribbling, Shadow is a good activity for participants in the sports of basketball, soccer, and field hockey.

How Many Participants?
Three or more pairs.

What Type of Equipment?
⑥ One ball for each person.

⑥ Any equipment specific to the sport.

Where?
Any defined area.

Safety Considerations
Ensure that participants can perform the basic skill required before commencing Shadow. Otherwise, people are so focused on trying to dribble the ball that they tend to collide with each other. In addition, when participants do not possess basic skills, there tend to be more loose balls.

Helpful Hints
⑥ After a set length of time, have the participants switch roles.

⑥ If you want to emphasize proper technique, have participants walk instead of run.

⑥ Make sure less-skilled individuals have more space than highly skilled individuals.

Extensions and Variations
⑥ Instead of dribbling a ball, participants can pass a volleyball to themselves or bounce a tennis ball or a birdie on a racket. Similarly, for water polo, swimmers can swim with a ball in front of them.

⑥ To make the activity more challenging for the follower, the leader is allowed to move without a ball.

10.3   STRIPTEASE

13+

The Basics

Basic ball-handling drills can be dull and monotonous. Nevertheless, sports participants need to practice them over and over until they can handle the ball without thinking. Striptease is a fun way of getting lots of touches on the ball while focusing on another task. Two people pass a ball back and forth to each other (the type of ball depends on the specific sport). While doing so, they take off their shoes and socks and put them back on. Participants are not allowed to touch their shoes or socks when the ball is not in play.

How Many Participants?

Two or more.

What Type of Equipment?

⊚ One ball for each pair.

⊚ Each person must be wearing shoes and socks.

Where?

Indoors is preferable.

Safety Considerations

⊚ People need to keep their eyes on the ball at all times, removing their socks and shoes by feel.

⊚ When shoes are off but socks are still on, there is a risk that participants may lose their footing if the playing surface is slippery. If this is the case, require that participants remove one shoe and sock before moving to the other shoe and sock.

Helpful Hints

Although obvious, it may be helpful to remind individuals that passing the ball high in the air allows more time for removing their footwear.

Extensions and Variations

Almost any ball sport that does not require participants to keep two hands on a stick, as in field hockey and lacrosse, can be used. For example, basketball, volleyball, netball, soccer, football, rugby, softball, baseball, and cricket can easily incorporate this activity. Striptease can also work in tennis or badminton, although tennis players would need to be very skilled.

10.4   KEEP IT ROLLING

8+

The Basics

Keep It Rolling works on basic ball-handling skills while dividing the participants' attention. As people become more skilled, the basic ball-handling skill (e.g., passing) becomes automatic. The addition of another task increases the challenge. In competitive situations, athletes often need to be able to perform a basic skill while thinking of, or preparing for, another skill.

In pairs, people stand and pass a ball back and forth (the type of ball depends on the specific sport). At the same time the participants roll another ball between them on the ground by bending down and pushing it with their hands. The challenge is to maintain control of the ball being passed in the air while keeping the ball on the ground moving at all times.

How Many Participants?
One or more pairs.

What Type of Equipment?
One ball for each person.

Where?
Any flat area.

Safety Considerations
The ball in the air should always be the primary focus of attention.

Helpful Hints
Encourage people to talk to each other to increase awareness of the location of the balls.

Extensions and Variations
⑥ Rather than rolling the ball on the ground by pushing it with the hands, have participants try kicking it or even making a bounce pass.

⑥ Keep a ball in the air. In soccer, while passing a ball on the ground to a partner, throw and catch a second ball.

⑥ Try Keep It Rolling in groups of three with three balls. For the highly skilled, try four balls with three people. The trio needs to keep two balls moving on the ground and two balls moving in the air. Establishing a set pattern of movement for the balls makes this version a bit less chaotic.

10.5   DO IT IN THE DARK

8+

The Basics

Individuals need to be aware of their current actions before they can successfully alter or improve their technique. Do It in the Dark helps people develop their kinesthetic awareness. This activity is intended for people who already understand the basic movement pattern of the skill. Have athletes perform a specified closed skill (i.e., one that does not require them to react to a ball or to someone else). Be sure to pick a skill that can be performed repetitively (e.g., tennis or volleyball serve, golf swing, dance move, basketball free throw, archery shot, discus throw, swimming start). Participants then perform the skill blindfolded.

How Many Participants?

One or more.

What Type of Equipment?

Implements from the relevant sport.

Where?

The appropriate location for the sport.

Safety Considerations

If objects are being thrown or hit, be sure to take precautions. When blindfolded, some individuals lose their sense of direction. It may be appropriate for participants to work in pairs, with one partner sighted and the other blindfolded.

Helpful Hints

Individuals should focus on the feel of the skill, not the outcome (e.g., whether or not the serve or the free throw was successful).

Extensions and Variations

⊚ Encourage participants to focus on different aspects of their bodies for each repetition. For example, have them begin by considering how the feet are in contact with the ground. They then focus on their ankles, knees, thighs, hips, stomach, back, shoulders, neck, and head.

⊚ To help the development of spatial or court awareness, have individuals stand in a particular spot, close their eyes, and then move to a specified location or line without looking.

10.6   SWAP IT

8+

The Basics

Swap It is another activity designed to enhance kinesthetic awareness. Experienced athletes are sometimes unaware of what they are doing because the movement has become automatic. When this happens, changes in technique are virtually impossible. Swap It helps people become aware of what is involved in a particular skill.

Select a sport skill that is asymmetrical (i.e., is right- or left-handed or -footed or involves turning to the left or right). Have participants perform the skill to the opposite side or use the opposite hand or foot than usual. Possible examples include spinning or jumping in the opposite direction in skating; shooting with the opposite hand or foot in soccer, basketball, water polo, netball, or ice hockey; spiking with the opposite arm in volleyball; playing a racket sport with the opposite hand; throwing with the opposite hand or batting from the opposite side in baseball, cricket, or softball; or swinging a golf club from the opposite side.

How Many Participants?

One or more.

What Type of Equipment?

Equipment required in the selected sport (golfers and ice hockey players will need to arrange to get equipment suited for their nondominant hand).

Where?
The appropriate location for the sport.

Safety Considerations
If the skill involves explosive movements, initial attempts to the opposite side need to begin slowly because participants have not yet developed their movement patterns.

Helpful Hints
⑥ Swap It is an excellent activity for coaches or teachers to do themselves. By doing the skill in the opposite direction or on the opposite side, they often find it easier to break down the skill or explain the processes actually involved.

⑥ Attempting a skill with the nondominant hand, leg, or side can make highly skilled individuals feel somewhat uncoordinated. This experience can help these individuals identify with the frustrations that people with poor coordination or physical disabilities might encounter.

Extensions and Variations
⑥ After performing Swap It, have participants return to the normal or preferred side. Ask each person to discover a minor (or major) modification they can make to their technique that might enhance their performance.

⑥ To increase awareness even more, divide participants into pairs. One partner provides coaching to the other. Insist that all comments be worded positively (i.e., the words "don't," "not," and "no" are not allowed).

⑥ Incorporate Swap It into practice game situations. People are allowed to pass, shoot, spike, or bat only with the nonpreferred hand.

Striking and Fielding Games

Aside from elite competition, the sports of baseball, softball, and cricket often result in uneven levels of participation. Although some individuals get a lot of action, others regularly get shuffled out to right field (in baseball) or long off (in cricket). The irony is that those with better skills get more practice, making those less skilled feel even more inadequate. The activities in this chapter demand that everyone be actively involved (standing still waiting for a ball to come your way once in a blue moon is not being actively involved). All participants will get more exercise and more skill practice and will most likely have more fun with these merry methods that mix batting, catching, and throwing than they do with the standard games themselves.

8+

11.1   TOUCH IT

The Basics

Fielders tend to spend a lot of time just standing around. Touch It requires everyone to be active and encourages teams to work together. A batter hits the ball. Instead of running around the bases (or between the wickets), the batter runs around everyone else on his or her team. Each complete circuit of the team results in a point. Everyone on the fielding team must touch the ball at the same time before the runner stops running. The people on the batting team are not allowed to interfere with the fielding of the ball. Each person on the batting team bats once. The teams then switch roles.

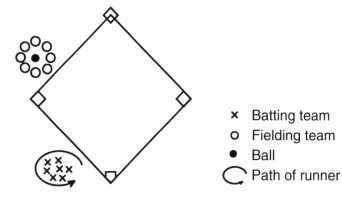

× Batting team
o Fielding team
• Ball
⌒ Path of runner

Touch It is a game that requires everyone to be active—whether they are fielding or waiting for a turn to bat.

How Many Participants?

Two teams of eight or more.

What Type of Equipment?

⑥ One bat.

⑥ One ball.

⑥ Fielder's gloves are optional.

⑥ Batting helmet (if appropriate).

Where?

A standard baseball or softball diamond or cricket oval.

Safety Considerations

If you're using Touch It in cricket, the rest of the batting team needs to be beyond the boundary until the ball has been hit. If you're using Touch It in softball or baseball, the rest of the batting team needs to be behind the backstop until the ball has been hit.

Helpful Hints

- ⑥ To avoid delays, either use a batting tee or allow teams to pitch (bowl) to themselves.
- ⑥ Encourage the fielding team to try different strategies. It may be that having everyone converge on the person who initially fields the ball is not the quickest method (particularly if the ball is hit into the outfield).
- ⑥ In baseball and softball, home runs that go out of the playing area are played over (no points are scored).
- ⑥ In cricket, 6's are played over (no points scored).

Extensions and Variations

- ⑥ Instead of everyone on the fielding team touching the ball at the same time, everyone must just touch it at some point. Therefore players can pass the ball between themselves rather than everyone running to the ball.
- ⑥ The fielding team must tunnel ball the ball back to the pitcher (see activity 9.1).
- ⑥ Batters can throw the ball instead of batting it.

11.2   CHARGE!

8+

● ●

The Basics

True to its name, Charge! involves the entire batting team charging to first base at the same time. Don't worry—no one can get called out at first! The main advantage of this activity is that members of the batting team are active while waiting for their turn at bat. Divide the group into two teams. Place a cone about 6 feet from first base in line with the baseline between first and second. As soon as the batter hits the ball, the entire batting team runs to first (or to the space between first base and the cone) and then back to home plate (not around the bases). When the fielding team gets the ball to the catcher, it gets 1 point for each runner who hasn't made it back to home plate (runners are forced out; they do not need to be tagged). This reverses the normal scoring procedure in that the fielding team, not the batting team, accumulates points. Each player bats once. The teams then switch roles.

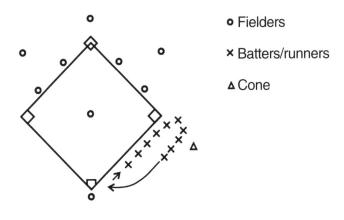

Charge! is another activity that keeps the entire batting team active and involved in the game.

How Many Participants?
Two teams of eight or more.

What Type of Equipment?
- One bat.
- One ball.
- One cone.
- Two bases.
- Fielder's gloves (if appropriate).
- Batting helmet (if appropriate).

Where?
Any standard baseball or softball diamond.

Safety Considerations
No sliding allowed.

Helpful Hints

- If the teams are large, consider having half the team run to first and back and the others to third and back. This eases congestion, except for that at home plate.
- Even if a fly ball is caught, no one is out until the ball gets to the catcher.
- Fielders need to keep thinking; they must overcome their automatic inclination to throw to first.

Extensions and Variations

To speed up the game, have the batting team pitch to itself (but still allow the fielding team to have someone standing by the pitching mound for fielding purposes). Allow each batter only two pitches. If the batter doesn't like the first pitch, he or she has to hit the second pitch. Alternatively, batters can hit the ball off a tee, eliminating pitching entirely.

11.3   BUCKET BRIGADE

8+

The Basics

Bucket Brigade is another fielding activity that stresses teamwork. Runners work on speed as they are awarded a point for every base. Everyone has to consider tactics. From home plate, one person throws three balls into the infield or outfield and then runs around the bases. The fielders need to put all three balls in a bucket placed at the pitcher's mound and then yell "Stop." The runner gets 1 point for each base touched before the fielders yell. Once that runner stops, he or she takes the place of someone in the field. This continues until everyone has had a turn as the runner. Runners keep track of their own score. Although there is no pitching in this game, someone still needs to be in the pitcher's position for fielding purposes.

How Many Participants?

Seven or more.

What Type of Equipment?

- Three balls.
- One bucket.
- Four bases.

Where?
Any standard baseball or softball diamond.

Safety Considerations
With three balls coming in to the pitcher at the same time, teams should consider having an infielder move in to the pitcher's mound to help field the balls into the bucket. Which infielder that is will obviously depend on where the balls have been thrown. Another alternative is to require that players roll the balls once they get to the infield.

Helpful Hints
If anyone on the fielding team yells "Stop" before all three balls are in the bucket, the runner receives an extra 3 points.

Extensions and Variations
Use Bucket Brigade as a team competition. If using teams it speeds things up (and keeps the batting team from twiddling their thumbs) if two people throw out two balls each. Both participants throw at the same time (to avoid potentially hitting a runner) and then begin to run more or less together. Rarely do two people run at the same speed, so one usually ends up in front of the other. As the runners are never tagged, and they never have to stop at a base, congestion is not an issue. Once everyone on the team has had a turn, teams switch. Working in pairs also allows people with weaknesses in running speed or throwing ability to experience greater success with the help of their partners.

11.4   DAVID AND GOLIATH

13+

The Basics
This activity requires accuracy as well as power in throwing. Have two lines about 50 feet apart. Divide the group into two teams. Each team lines up slightly behind their line, facing the center. Place a large ball (e.g., volleyball or beach ball) in the center of the playing area. Each player has a tennis ball. The objective for each team is to move the larger ball to the opposition's line by hitting the large ball with the tennis balls. Any tennis ball that crosses the line can be picked up and thrown again. If players can reach a tennis ball in the playing area without touching or crossing the line, they can reach over the line and pick

it up. Players are not allowed to touch the large ball (or the line). At no time are people allowed in the playing area. The target is always moving and is at varying distances, so the monotony of "playing catch" is avoided. Unlike many throwing activities, a single individual throw is not under scrutiny; the combination of multiple throws is the only outcome of interest.

How Many Participants?
Four or more.

What Type of Equipment?
⑥ One large ball (e.g., volleyball or beach ball).

⑥ One tennis ball for each participant.

Where?
A gym or enclosed tennis court.

Safety Considerations
⑥ Participants must warm up their shoulders before the start of this game.

⑥ When the large ball gets close to an end line, the defensive players (trying to keep the ball from crossing their line) need to be alert to the barrage of tennis balls that may be at their feet. Anyone who throws a tennis ball so that it crosses the opposition's line without touching the floor is given a suitable penalty (e.g., sitting down for 3 minutes or collecting all of the balls).

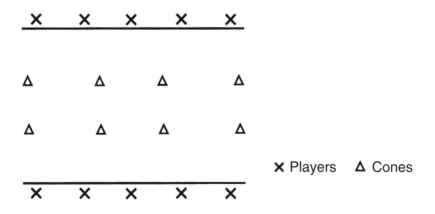

In the cone version of David and Goliath, throwers try to knock down the cones in the line farthest from them. The team that knocks down all the cones first wins.

Helpful Hints

⊚ If a lot of tennis balls accumulate in the playing area, call a 30-second truce and allow everyone to retrieve as many as they can. The leader may want to guard the large ball during the truce so no one "accidentally" moves it one way or the other.

⊚ Individuals in wheelchairs can easily be included in this activity. Often their enhanced upper-body strength makes them effective team members.

Extensions and Variations

⊚ Have two or more large balls in the center. A team wins when two large balls cross the line. As soon as a large ball crosses a line it is out of play.

⊚ Players aim to knock down cones rather than move a large ball. Set up two lines of cones, each line about 10 feet away from a line of throwers. The throwers aim to knock down the cones in the line farther away from them. A team wins when all of the cones in the opposite line are knocked down.

11.5   EXPERIENCE IT ALL

8+

The Basics

Experience It All allows everyone to play every position. This not only lets people practice different skills but also helps players develop an appreciation for the challenges involved in every position. Even within elite teams, players sometimes tend to think that their position is more difficult or demanding than everyone else's. When players experience the other positions and perhaps make an error or two, they may be less likely to judge or criticize their teammates.

Four or five players are initially batters. Nine players fill the positions in the field. As in normal baseball or softball, when the batters hit and run, the team on the field tries to get them out. After making an out, the batter moves to right field, right field moves to center, center to left, left to third, third to short, short to second, second to first, first to pitcher, pitcher to catcher, and the catcher becomes a batter. Players continue to bat as long as they do not make an out.

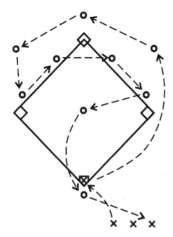

o Fielders

× Batters

Experience It All is unique in that it allows all participants an opportunity to play every position.

How Many Participants?
Twelve to 14 players.

What Type of Equipment?
ⓖ One bat.

ⓖ One ball.

ⓖ Four bases.

ⓖ Fielder's gloves.

ⓖ Catcher's equipment.

ⓖ Batting helmet.

Where?
Any standard baseball or softball diamond.

Safety Considerations
The standard safety concerns of softball and baseball apply. Another consideration might be that people who are used to playing the outfield may be a bit ball shy when playing at the catcher's or pitcher's position.

Helpful Hints
The teacher or coach may choose to pitch to all players, providing a consistent quality of pitching. Alternatively, batters can hit off a tee.

Extensions and Variations
ⓖ For a brain bender, play in the opposite direction than normal—first base becomes third and third becomes first.

ⓖ You can apply the same basic principles of Experience It All to cricket.

11.6   ADD-A-BALL

8+

The Basics

Add-a-Ball is based on throwing and catching and caters to groups of any ability level. Participants must throw accurately and be continually alert in this game. Five people stand in a circle facing each other. Give one person the ball, which is then thrown in a star pattern. Once the participants have established the pattern, introduce another ball. If the group adapts to the additional ball, add another.

How Many Participants?

Groups of five or more.

What Type of Equipment?

At least three balls for each group.

Where?

Anywhere!

Safety Considerations

When the group is first establishing the throwing pattern, it may be helpful if players call the name of the person they are throwing to just before they throw the ball. This may help alert players who are slow to identify the pattern.

→ Path of ball × Players

In this variation of Add-a-Ball, players have created a star passing pattern.

Helpful Hints

If someone drops a ball, the group starts again with one ball.

Extensions and Variations

- Five or more people stand in a circle and randomly create their own pattern by throwing the ball to anyone they want, but each person can receive the ball only once during the pattern. Once the pattern is established, balls are slowly added.

- Add-a-Ball is not limited to fielding and striking sports. You can adapt this activity to any sport that involves passing (e.g., lacrosse, volleyball, rugby, netball, football, basketball, or water polo).

11.7   CONTINUOUS CHALLENGE

13+

The Basics

Continuous Challenge is ideal for keeping skilled, experienced players entertained and alert. Create two equal teams. One team bats and the other fields. Place a target and a cone about 15 feet apart. A pitcher pitches the ball toward the target. At all times the pitcher must stay within a designated zone (e.g., on the pitching mound). The first batter defends the target by hitting the ball. Fielders must field foul balls as well as fair ones, but a batter is only allowed one foul ball before being out (a second foul ball is an automatic out). There is no catcher. After hitting the ball, the batter runs back and forth between the target and the cone as many times as possible, earning 1 point for each round trip. If the pitch is inaccurate and not hittable, the batter can still earn points by running back and forth between the target and the cone while someone retrieves the ball and throws it to the pitcher. Fielders must return the ball to the pitcher, who immediately pitches toward the target again. The pitcher can pitch the ball while the batter is still running between the target and the cone, trying to hit the target while the batter isn't there to protect it. The batter is out if a fly ball is caught, or if the ball hits the target but only if thrown by the pitcher. As soon as one batter is out, the next batter immediately retrieves the bat (only one bat is in use during the game) and begins to defend the target and run; the fielding team does not need to wait for the next batter. If the pitcher hits the target before the next batter is ready, that batter is out before getting to the plate; whoever is on deck has to be ready at all times. The teams switch roles when everyone on the batting team has been out.

o   Fielders

×   Batters/runners

△   Cone

◎   Target

In Continuous Challenge (shown here with a right-handed batter), the batter runs back and forth between the target and the cone after hitting the ball. One point is earned for each round trip.

How Many Participants?
Two teams of 6 to 11 players each.

What Type of Equipment?
- One target. The batter stands where the umpire normally does; you can easily place the target on the backstop, slightly lower than the standard strike zone. A trash can lid tied to the backstop is one possibility.
- One cone (two if both left- and right-handed batters are playing).
- One bat.
- One ball.
- Fielder's gloves (optional).
- Batting helmet.

Where?
Standard softball or baseball diamond.

Safety Considerations
Players can get so involved in this game that they forget safety considerations. The main safety issue is the potential of the pitch to hit a batter/runner returning to home plate. Caution the batter to be very aware of the speed and direction of the incoming pitch. Have left-handed batters run to a cone placed on the other side of the target.

Helpful Hints
- Vary the pitcher.
- It can be useful to begin with a softer ball so players become aware of the rules without worrying about safety.

Extensions and Variations
- Cricket variation: use a cricket oval instead of a baseball or softball diamond. There is a bowler instead of a pitcher. There is no such thing as a foul ball. A standard wicket is used for the target.
- On rainy days participants can play Continuous Challenge indoors in a gym with either a foam ball and a regular bat or with a plastic bat and ball. All rules remain the same.
- You can also use Continuous Challenge with field hockey or soccer. Individuals arrange themselves in the field as in baseball. The target can be a trash can behind home plate. Strikers (instead of batters) trap and drive (field hockey) or trap and kick (soccer) the ball into the infield or outfield. The only real change to the rules is that the ball must stay on the ground at all times.

Invasion
Games

Invasion sports include any sport where the ball can be intercepted by the opposition (e.g., soccer, netball, basketball, hockey, and touch football). This section contains a mixture of tried-and-true activities (some of which readers will recognize) as well as some unusual, more inventive games. We have found that sometimes the familiar options get overlooked, or group leaders do not consider the variations of these standard games. When trying out the games in this section, we found the participants reacted with great competitive spirit to both the activities they may have played during recess as kids as well as the new games.

This chapter contains amusing antics for the active application of attacking techniques (and defense, too)!

12.1 PSEUDO SOCCER

8+

The Basics

Pseudo Soccer can serve as an excellent warm-up activity for any sport. Specific soccer skills are not an advantage, but an understanding of soccer tactics and strategies is helpful. Pseudo Soccer is also a good conditioning exercise. Create a playing area that is smaller than a standard soccer field. The exact size will depend on the number of players. Divide the group into two equal teams and have them play soccer, but with two major rule changes: only hands can touch the ball, and the ball must remain in contact with the ground at all times.

How Many Participants?

Two teams of three or more.

What Type of Equipment?

One ball (soccer balls or volleyballs work best).

Where?

Indoors or outdoors in an area designated by lines. A volleyball court (without the net) works well for teams of three to five players. Larger teams will need a larger area.

Safety Considerations

Encourage people to bend their knees to reach the ball rather than just bending at the waist (this helps prevent sore backs).

Helpful Hints

⑥ Pseudo Soccer is more tiring than it appears. Leaders should limit periods to no more than 5 minutes.

⑥ If playing indoors, participants can play the ball off the walls. This avoids dead time when people have to retrieve the ball.

Extensions and Variations

⑥ Crab soccer: everyone assumes the crab position (stomach facing up, moving on hands and feet). People cannot touch the ball if their backsides are in contact with the ground. Players can use their hands or feet to move the ball.

⑥ Three-legged soccer: normal soccer rules apply, but each player is tied at one ankle to a partner. They can kick with either their individual feet or their big combined foot. Goalies can be tied around the waist back-to-back.

⑥ Blindfold soccer: players pair up—one person is blindfolded, the other can see. Through verbal communication, the pairs try to intercept the ball that is being passed between three or more other sighted people. Have at least as many pairs as there are individual sighted players.

12.2   PICK A HAND

13+

The Basics

Pick a Hand is appropriate for invasion sports that usually involve the use of both hands (e.g., basketball, netball, touch football). Challenge athletes to control the ball with only one hand. This often results in the development of methods of ball control that they might not otherwise use. Regardless of the sport, all players place their nonpreferred hand behind their backs. They are not allowed to use that arm and hand in any way.

How Many Participants?

Two to 30 (depending on the sport).

What Type of Equipment?

Standard equipment for the sport involved.

Where?

Standard playing area for the sport involved.

Safety Considerations

For sports that involve balls being passed above the waist, players need to be alert for a ball approaching the face at high speed, because they have only one arm to defend themselves with instead of two.

Helpful Hints

For athletes who have difficulty keeping their arms behind their backs, either have them tuck that hand in their shorts or sweats, or loosely tie the arm to the waist.

Extensions and Variations

◎ Require that each participant play with their nondominant hand.

◎ If a range of ability levels exists within a given group, have the more-skilled players play with their nondominant hand while everyone else plays with their dominant hand.

12.3   GET IT FIRST

8+

The Basics

Sometimes known as Steal the Bacon or Dog and Bone, Get It First is a game that people often forget after elementary school. Although developed as a game for recess, Get It First is an excellent method of practicing attacking and defensive skills. The basic rules can apply to any invasion sport. Divide the group into two teams. Have two lines approximately 50 feet apart. Each team lines up on one of these sidelines. Have both teams count off and remember their numbers. Set up goal areas at each end line and establish which goal belongs to which team. Place a ball in the center of the playing area. The leader calls out two or more numbers. The players with those numbers have the objective of scoring in the opponent's goal using whatever techniques are appropriate for the specific sport. Obviously, whoever reaches the ball first and gains control of it becomes the offensive team.

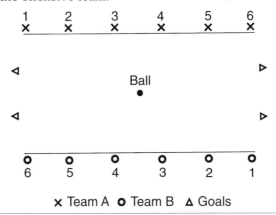

Starting position for Get It First. This game can be used with most invasion sports, such as basketball, hockey, or soccer.

How Many Participants?
Two teams of four or more.

What Type of Equipment?
⑥ One ball and any equipment required in the sport involved—for example, field hockey sticks.

⑥ Two goals. Setting up two cones to make one goal works well.

Where?
Indoors or outdoors in a defined area.

Safety Considerations
If a tussle begins over initial ownership of the ball, all players return to the sidelines and different numbers are called.

Helpful Hints
The leader may want to introduce a time limit for each goal attempt so those on the sidelines do not get bored.

Extensions and Variations
⑥ Require that the ball be passed at least once (or twice or three times) before an attempt can be made on the goal.

⑥ Players whose numbers have been called can involve the players on the sidelines by passing them the ball. The players on the sidelines must remain in place.

12.4   KEEP AWAY KAPERS

8+

The Basics
Many kids play keep away during recess. The basic concepts of keep away can apply to all invasion sports, requiring participants to work on ball control and interception skills. Divide players into groups of three. One person is in the middle and the other two pass the ball back and forth. The two people passing the ball need to remain in defined areas. The person in the middle tries to intercept the ball. When the ball is intercepted, the last person who touched it goes into the middle. Instead of just throwing the ball back and forth, participants use the skills and

techniques appropriate for their particular sport. For example, field hockey players trap and push the ball, soccer players trap and kick, and basketball players bounce pass.

How Many Participants?
Groups of three or more.

What Type of Equipment?
◎ One ball for each group.

◎ Equipment appropriate to the specific sport.

Where?
Indoors or outdoors.

Safety Considerations
To protect vertically challenged individuals from total frustration in sports where the ball can be passed in the air, stipulate that all passes be no higher than 2 feet above the person's head (when both feet are on the ground, not at the top of their jump).

Helpful Hints
◎ The smaller the area in which each person is allowed to move, the more difficult it is for the passers.

◎ If you see participants using delay tactics, limit the length of time any one person can hold the ball.

Extensions and Variations
◎ Place a time limit on the activity. Each person tries to intercept the ball as many times as possible within the given period.

◎ Play in teams. Within a defined playing area, players can stand or move wherever they want. To score a point, each team must pass the ball 10 times within their team without the ball being touched by the opposition. If the ball is touched but remains under the control of the same team, the team begins counting again from one. If the ball is intercepted, the team that intercepted it begins passing the ball within their team and counting.

12.5   STOP AND HOARD

8+

The Basics

Stop and Hoard is an excellent game for practicing individual defense and can be used with any sport that has a goalkeeper (e.g., field or ice hockey, soccer, lacrosse, or water polo). In each group of five or six, assign one person to be the defender. All of the other players have a ball each and are attackers. The defender has two aims: to defend the goal and to collect balls. The defender can knock away balls if he or she does not have the time or position to actually collect the ball. Designate a space or location for collected balls. Attackers are not allowed to re-trieve balls once they have been collected but otherwise are free to use any ball that has been knocked away. When the defender has collected half the balls, someone else defends and the previous defender becomes an attacker. All balls are released from the collection area whenever a new defender takes over.

How Many Participants?

Groups of five or six.

What Type of Equipment?

- ⊚ Five balls (or pucks) for a group of six; four balls (or pucks) for a group of five.
- ⊚ Standard equipment for the particular sport.
- ⊚ Designated goal area.
- ⊚ Designated ball collection area.

Where?

A flat area.

Safety Considerations

- ⊚ In sports where players wear protective equipment, ensure that each new defender is wearing all of the appropriate gear before the first attack is launched.
- ⊚ When first attempting Stop and Hoard, either decrease the num-ber of balls available or replace standard balls with softer alterna-tives.

Helpful Hints

⑥ If a high number of goals are being scored, retrieving the balls for further play becomes time-consuming and even dangerous. Instead of retrieving the balls already in the goal, have a supply of additional balls for the attackers to use.

⑥ Because the defender is definitely outnumbered, require that all offensive players begin their attack from a designated point.

⑥ Rather than all attackers approaching the goalie at the same moment, stagger the offense. Instead of being confronted with four or five balls at once, the defender deals with a continual barrage, one ball after another.

Extensions and Variations

⑥ The defender loses a ball out of the collection area for every two goals that are scored.

⑥ Instead of shooting at the goal, the attackers need to dribble their balls from one side of a defined area to the other (the goal area is no longer part of the game). The defender still has the job of collecting a predetermined number of balls. If an attacker's ball is collected, then that person remains on offense, available to receive passes from other attackers. Two defenders can join forces and work together to collect balls from the offensive players.

12.6   SPACE INVADERS

13+

The Basics

Space Invaders is designed to work on participants' ball-handling skills and accuracy. Each player moves a ball through a course while being aware of potential sabotage from the sidelines. Space Invaders is appropriate for any sport that involves dribbling. Set up a line of five to eight cones spaced approximately 3 feet apart. Each player has a ball. One person dribbles a ball through the line of cones. The other players are on the sidelines and attempt to hit the person's ball with their balls. Any ball that makes it past the opposite line can be put into play again by the people on the sidelines.

How Many Participants?

Groups of 5 to 15.

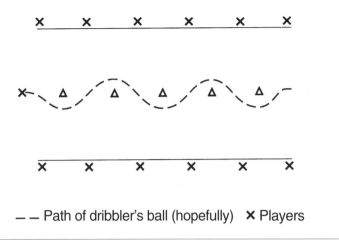

— — Path of dribbler's ball (hopefully)   ✕ Players

Space Invaders requires a dribbler to make it through the line of cones without having his or her ball hit by the balls of the sideline players.

What Type of Equipment?
- One ball for each player.
- Equipment appropriate for the specific sport.
- Five to eight cones.

Where?
A flat area.

Safety Considerations
- For soccer and hockey, all balls must stay on the ground at all times.
- For field hockey, restrict players to pushes rather than hits on the ball.
- For ice hockey, slap shots are not allowed.

Helpful Hints
- The distance between the sidelines and the cones should be determined by the participants' skill level.
- In basketball, the players on the sidelines should use bounce passes to try to disrupt the dribbler.

Extensions and Variations
- Place a time limit on each dribbler.
- Place the cones in a circle surrounded by the rest of the team (a circle within a circle). This arrangement increases the difficulty because balls can come from any direction at any time.

12.7   CROQUET CONCEPTS

8+

The Basics

Croquet Concepts focuses on accuracy rather than power, speed, interceptions, or strength. The stationary aspect of this game allows the hidden talents of budding pool sharks, physicists, and other angle-oriented individuals to excel. The game is appropriate for any sport that involves passing or hitting a ball along the ground (e.g., field hockey, soccer, or putting in golf). Set up the field with a series of targets in a defined pattern. Targets should be at least 15 feet apart. Each player has a ball. Taking turns, players get a single hit or kick of the ball to try to hit the first target. If they hit it, they get another turn immediately. If they miss a target, it is the next person's turn. The goal is to make it through the course, hitting each successive target in turn, as quickly as possible. Players always have the option of using their turn to knock a competitor's ball away from a target (or into oblivion). As in golf, every attempt to move the ball counts as a turn (stroke).

How Many Participants?

Two to five on each course.

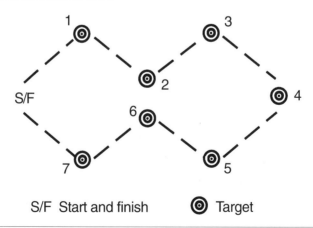

S/F Start and finish   ◎ Target

Accuracy is the focus of Croquet Concepts—rather than strength, power, or speed.

What Type of Equipment?

- ❻ One ball for each person.
- ❻ Targets: hoops, sticks in the ground, cones.
- ❻ Equipment required for the particular sport.

Where?

Indoors or outdoors.

Safety Considerations

All participants need to keep their attention on the game, even when it isn't their turn. Balls can end up almost anywhere. Not only should players avoid being hit, but they also have to keep track of their balls!

Helpful Hints

- ❻ Players can use colored chalk to give their balls a unique identity. Otherwise, find some other way to identify individual balls.
- ❻ Limit the number of players to five. With any more than five, players spend too much time standing around.

Extensions and Variations

- ❻ Have participants play in pairs.
- ❻ Play Goofy Golf instead of croquet: players are not allowed to hit other balls out of the way, and the number of "strokes" for each target or "hole" is recorded.

Net Games

This chapter of novel net notions is designed for the sports of volley-ball, tennis, badminton, and table tennis. In addition to skill, net games require considerable concentration. Most of the activities in this section alter the perspective of the game, demanding continual attention and diverse tactics. Participants soon expect the unexpected, resulting in enhanced anticipation and sharpened reflexes.

13.1   COVER UP

13+

The Basics

Rarely are athletes aware of the visual cues they rely on in their sport. Rather than having blindfolded athletes (which becomes problematic in sports where balls fly silently through the air), in Cover Up part of the visual field is obscured. Tactics change and reactions are challenged because players are not able to see the ball at all times. Place sheets, towels, or a tarp over the net so that no one can see through it. Play as usual.

How Many Participants?

Numbers normally used in the sport (e.g., 2 or 4 in tennis and 4 to 12 in volleyball).

What Type of Equipment?

⑥ Sheets, large towels, or a tarp.

⑥ Standard equipment needed for the particular sport.

Where?

Any standard court normally used for the specific sport.

Safety Considerations

Particularly in volleyball, be sure that the cloth covering the net remains at least 2 feet off the ground. Although the game is more challenging when the visual space underneath the net is covered, dangling cloths can be deadly when feet get caught in them.

Helpful Hints

⑥ Cover Up is not particularly effective for table tennis.

⑥ Having a "Cover Up Volleyball" tournament, using the format described here, can be a fun way of raising money for a school or club team.

Extensions and Variations

Have one person on each team stationed so that he or she can see under or around the net. Let this person try to help out the team by giving verbal information about what no one else can see. Allowing the team to discuss what information is useful and how players can convey it in a short time is a useful communication exercise.

13.2   CONTINUAL RALLY

8+

The Basics
Continual Rally emphasizes cooperation through ball control. The activity gets progressively more difficult in that replacing oxygen becomes more important than placing the ball. Have two lines of participants, one on each side of the net. After a player hits the ball over the net, he or she runs around the net (or table) and joins the line on the other side. The object is to keep the rally going rather than to score a point.

How Many Participants?
Numbers depend on the sport. In table tennis, Continual Rally can be attempted with three people. For tennis, it is unrealistic to try it with fewer than five. Even with more people, however, heart rates remain high.

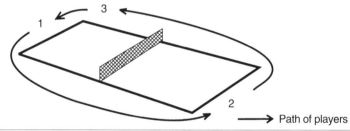

The table tennis variation of Continual Relay (above) requires just as much concentration and cardiovascular endurance as other net sport versions of the game.

What Type of Equipment?
Standard equipment for the sport involved.

Where?
Any standard court or table normally used for the specific sport.

Safety Considerations
On courts where one raises the net by winding a crank, be sure the crankshaft is either removed or heavily padded. This activity is not appropriate for old-fashioned courts on which wire stays hold up the net.

Helpful Hints
You may need to remind players that hitting the ball (or birdie) higher gives the next person in line more time to return it.

Extensions and Variations

- For volleyball, Continuous Rally can be a simple passing or setting exercise over the net. Alternatively, it is good practice for the setter's movement skills (and fitness) to have one setter set the teams on both sides by running back and forth under the net. This alternative works best with a total of five players.

- For racket or paddle sports, make Continual Rally more difficult by having only one racket for each side. Players need time to pass the racket to the next person.

13.3   QUARTER THE COURT

8+

The Basics

It is amazing how players need to adjust their perspectives and skills when one aspect of the game is changed. Quarter the Court is no exception. On a normal court, place another net or a brightly colored rope or cord across the middle of the net so the court is divided into quarters. Instead of two teams, there are four! Teams can hit the ball to any of the other three teams. Teams do not need to have served to win a point. The team that wins the point serves.

How Many Participants?

Four teams. In table tennis, badminton, or tennis, teams of one player will work; volleyball requires a minimum of two people for each team.

What Type of Equipment?

- Normal equipment required for the specific sport.
- A second net or piece of bright-colored rope.
- Something to which the second net or the rope can be tied.

Where?

Any standard court (or table) normally used for the specific sport.

Safety Considerations

Many people are conditioned to expect the ball to come from only one direction. Reminding them to always keep their eyes on the ball (or the birdie) can help prevent unexpected bonks on the head.

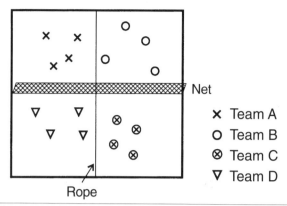

× Team A
○ Team B
⊗ Team C
▽ Team D

Net

Rope

In Quarter the Court, players may receive balls from three other teams rather than one, so concentration and attention are important.

Helpful Hints

In tennis, the rope or second net can be tied to the fence. In badminton and volleyball, a second net can be tied to additional poles or rope can be tied to walls (or trees if playing outdoors). In table tennis you can tie a string or the second net to the backs of high-backed chairs.

Extensions and Variations

Add a second ball. Because four teams are playing at all times, with only one ball in play, three teams will be waiting to see if that one ball is hit to them. With two balls in play at once, participants have to expand their focus of attention and be aware of both balls at the same time. Adding a second ball works best if two teams serve a ball to the teams not serving. After the serve, teams can hit either ball to any of the three teams. If the rally with one ball finishes, the ball is cleared off the court and not retrieved until the rally with the second ball has finished. With two balls, scoring happens twice as fast, so you might consider appointing specific players to act as score keepers.

13.4 TARGET PRACTICE

8+

The Basics

Net games require serves to go in before people can play. As the level of competition increases, the effectiveness of the serve can directly impact the outcome of the game. A common problem is that repetitive serving, although necessary, is often boring. Target Practice helps to keep boredom at bay while enhancing accuracy. Place a target on the court. Participants try to hit the target as many times as possible given a specified number of serves.

How Many Participants?
One or more.

What Type of Equipment?
- A target. The specific target depends on the sport—a target used in table tennis would be ludicrous for volleyball, and vice versa! Small plastic cups make good targets for table tennis. Chairs work well for volleyball, a folded towel works for badminton, and a pile of tennis balls (one ball balanced on top of three others) does the trick in tennis.
- Normal equipment required for the specific sport.

Where?
Any standard court (or table) normally used for the specific sport.

Safety Considerations
If people are serving from both sides of the court at the same time, each server needs to follow his or her serve visually to be able to verbally forewarn potential ball magnets (some people tend to attract balls!).

Helpful Hints
- The less skilled the athletes are, the bigger the target should be.
- Motivation tends to increase when there is an obvious result of hitting a target (e.g., it makes a loud noise or, better yet, something falls over).

Extensions and Variations
- Have more than one target, with different targets worth different point values.
- Instantly increase participants' motivation and intensity of effort by making yourself the target (obviously, this is not appropriate for table tennis). Note: having the teacher or coach act as a target might be against particular schools' or programs' policies. Activity leaders should take care to follow the appropriate policies.
- Devise a scoring system—1 point for getting the ball in the court, 5 points for hitting the target. The first person to reach 25 points wins!

13.5   MINI COURT

8+

The Basics
When the size or shape of a court changes, players need to change their tactics. When the court is smaller than normal, players must emphasize ball control. Shorten or limit the width of the court. Play as usual.

How Many Participants?
Two or more.

What Type of Equipment?
⑥ Line markers.

⑥ Normal equipment required for the specific sport.

Where?
It is often easiest to modify an existing court. For example, in tennis you can just declare that the service line is the end line. In table tennis, place a net across one-half of an old table, or across a coffee table (and play sitting down!).

Safety Considerations
If the normal number of players participates and the court is made smaller, overcrowding may result in unintentional contact. Emphasize the importance of communication.

Helpful Hints
With a smaller court, it may be appropriate to decrease the number of participants.

Extensions and Variations
⑥ Instead of shortening the court, keep the normal length but make the court narrower.

⑥ When there is more than one person on each side, require everyone to change or rotate positions after each rally or each time the ball (or birdie) crosses the net.

13.6   TWO BALLS (BIRDIES) AT ONCE

13+

The Basics

In Two Balls at Once, things happen twice as fast as in a normal game. This is an ideal activity for adrenaline junkies and those with quick reflexes. Both teams (or people) serve at the same time. Play continues as usual—there is just twice as much of it!

How Many Participants?

Standard-sized teams used in the specific sport.

What Type of Equipment?

⑥ Normal equipment required for the specific sport.

⑥ One extra ball (or birdie).

Where?

Any standard court (or table) normally used for the specific sport.

Safety Considerations

Rarely do both balls travel at the same speed, so at times players have two balls approaching them at the same time. A broad focus of attention is necessary—players who take the time to admire a well-placed shot may *feel* the second ball before they see it!

Helpful Hints

⑥ You can structure the scoring so that each ball is worth 1 point, or one ball is worth twice as many points as the other.

⑥ In tennis, everyone starts with their second serve, so service faults do not need to be taken into account.

Extensions and Variations

⑥ Instead of both teams or players serving at the same time, one player serves two balls in succession, putting both balls into play.

⑥ For team sports, give two "hot potatoes" (extra balls) to each side. These hot potatoes can never touch the ground. Players cannot touch the ball being rallied if they are holding a hot potato. Instead, they must quickly pass the hot potato before playing the ball.

Water Games

The activities in this chapter can cater to both swimmers and nonswimmers. The teacher or coach needs to be aware of the swimming competence of the participants before moving a group to an activity requiring swimming ability. Some of the activities can be enjoyed by both barnacles (those who are only comfortable clinging to the side in deep water) and barracudas (those who seem as if they were born in the water). Please remember that these water games are not restricted to use by swimming teachers and coaches only. Landlubbers can use water games as a form of cross-training (and just for fun!). We hope you enjoy these wet, wild, and wacky ways for working in water.

13+

14.1 UNDERWATER TAG

● ●

The Basics

Many of the tag games described in chapter 3 can be adapted to water. Underwater Tag, however, is unique to water (oddly enough!) and has not been depicted previously. One or more people are designated as It. Everyone must remain in the pool. Standard tag rules apply, with the addition that It cannot tag anyone who is completely submerged. It can tag only those parts of the body that are above the water.

How Many Participants?

Five or more.

What Type of Equipment?

No equipment needed!

Where?

A pool or other defined swimming area.

Safety Considerations

If nonswimmers are part of the group, make sure the entire designated area is shallow enough for them to be able to stand.

Helpful Hints

To identify which people in the pool are It, require those who are It to carry an object.

Extensions and Variations

⑥ When people are tagged, they must spin around 360 degrees before setting out to tag others.

⑥ Body tag: Decide which body part has to be tagged (e.g., foot, right hand). That body part can be tagged above or under the water.

14.2   POLO PLUS

13+

The Basics

Polo Plus is an excellent activity for people who know how to swim. It promotes water confidence, water skills, and cardiovascular fitness. Participants soon find out why water polo games are limited to 5-minute quarters. Polo Plus can serve as a fun break from the gym, field, or even swimming lanes and is an ideal summer activity for people in any sport. Use standard water polo rules and equipment but allow all swimmers to wear flippers. As a quick reminder, here are a few of the basic water polo rules.

- The game begins with the teams lined up at the goal lines. When the referee throws the ball in the middle of the pool, the players are free to move to obtain the ball.
- Players (except for the goalies) may touch the ball with only one hand at any one time.
- Players are not allowed to push off the bottom or sides of the pool.
- Players cannot take the ball entirely under the surface of the water.
- Goalies may not throw the ball past halfway.
- After a goal, players may be anywhere within their half, with the nonscoring side in possession of the ball.
- No one is allowed to touch a player who is not actually in contact with the ball.

How Many Participants?

Four to 14.

What Type of Equipment?

- One water polo ball or equivalent.
- Two goals.
- Identifying caps.
- One pair of flippers for each swimmer.

Where?

Deep end of a swimming pool.

Safety Considerations

⊚ Polo Plus is designed for swimmers. You can adapt the game for nonswimmers by situating it in the shallow end of the pool; however, this greatly decreases the cardiovascular demand. If the game takes place in the shallow end, do not have participants wear flippers.

⊚ When wearing flippers, participants have greater speed and can keep their bodies higher above the water than they can without flippers. Because of these increased dynamics, it may be appropriate to ban all body contact. This will not actually stop all body contact, but it will make it easier to enforce a game free from unwanted rough play.

Helpful Hints

Use PVC pipes or foam tubes to make lightweight and relatively inexpensive goals.

Extensions and Variations

⊚ For skilled groups, require that everyone on the team touch the ball before the team attempts a goal.

⊚ Inner tube water polo: each participant sits in an inner tube. Anyone in possession of the ball is fair game for being dumped from their tube. No one is allowed to touch the ball, opponents, or other tubes if they are not in their tube, and no one is allowed to touch anyone who doesn't have the ball.

14.3   WACKY RELAYS

8+

The Basics

Some of the relays in chapter 9 can be adapted for the water. For example, you can adapt activity 9.5 (Progressive Relay) by giving each team a surfboard (i.e., beginning with one person, each team adds another person to the board after each lap). Wacky Relays are activities designed specifically for the aquatic environment. Within each team, each participant finds a partner. One person provides the arm action and the other holds that person's feet or legs and kicks. Each pair swims to the other end of the pool, switches positions, and swims back.

How Many Participants?
Eight or more.

What Type of Equipment?
No equipment needed!

Where?
Any swimming area.

Safety Considerations
- The swimmer performing the kicking action often ends up underwater. Pairs may want to consider doing the backstroke.
- It may be helpful to pair weaker swimmers with stronger swimmers.

Helpful Hints
- Having the arms-only person use a pullbuoy may make the activity easier for the kicker.
- If there is an odd number of people in the relays involving pairs, one person goes twice (with a different partner each time).

Extensions and Variations
- Underwater leapfrog: one person stands with his or her legs apart; the partner swims between that person's legs and as far as possible underwater before standing, keeping in mind that the partner needs to be able to reach that spot in one breath. Partners alternate until they reach the end of the course. Although this is a shallow-water activity, it is best restricted to swimmers.
- Dragging relay: one person grasps the partner under the armpits and drags him or her backward. Partners switch for the return. Best done in shallow water. Appropriate for nonswimmers.
- T-shirt relay: provide each team with a large T-shirt. Individuals must have the shirt on to swim their leg of the relay.
- Retrieval relay: place a plastic container with a screw-top lid in deep water. Place as many lightweight objects in the container as there are relay participants, ensuring that the container will still float. The participants' challenge is to swim to the container, unscrew the lid (without letting water into the container), select an object, rescrew the lid, swim back, and tag the next person.

14.4   DIFFICULT DARES

8+

The Basics

Set up Difficult Dares as a group circuit or as individual challenges. This can serve as a great cross-training activity in that it provides a variety of exercises in a nonimpact environment. Participation in water activities has been shown to enhance recovery for people in land-based sports more effectively than just taking a break from training. Create an activity circuit. Stations can include any or all of the following.

⊚ Push-ups against the side of the pool.

⊚ Push-ups on the bottom of the pool (more difficult than it sounds).

⊚ Swimming in place with the partner holding the ankles.

⊚ Treading water (with hands on head).

⊚ Sitting or lying down on the bottom of the pool.

⊚ Running across the pool (shallow end).

⊚ Sculling on the back, feetfirst (or headfirst).

⊚ Turning somersaults (forward or backward).

⊚ Jumping across the pool (shallow or deep end).

⊚ Piggyback your partner across the pool.

How Many Participants?

Two or more.

What Type of Equipment?

No equipment needed!

Where?

Swimming pool.

Safety Considerations

The specific makeup of stations should depend on the swimming ability of the participants. It is possible to create both shallow-water and deepwater stations.

Helpful Hints

⊚ Water is a friendly environment for many people with physical disabilities. Many of the stations in Difficult Dares need minimal

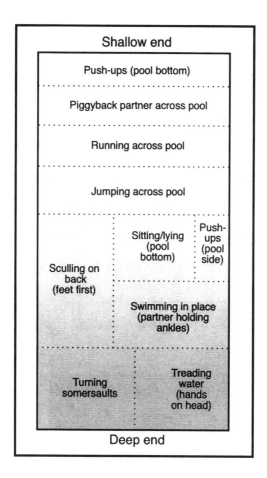

The specific makeup of your group's Difficult Dares stations should be tailored to participants' swimming abilities and fitness levels.

adaptation to include people with mild or moderate physical disabilities. Of course, paraplegics cannot run across the pool or give piggyback rides to their partners, but they can easily scull, swim, play catch, do upper-body exercises such as dips on the side of the pool, and tread water.

6 In many instances a participant, for whatever reason, will be unable to go in the water on a particular day. Include this person in Difficult Dares by setting up a station that involves interaction between someone in the pool and someone on land. For example, require the swimmer to kick a ball out of the deep end to the land-based person a specified number of times.

⑥ If using Difficult Dares in a competitive sport environment rather than an exercise environment, making the stations competitive can create greater enthusiasm. At each station individuals can compete to see who can successfully complete the activity first (for treading water, the competition might be who can get themselves highest out of the water).

Extensions and Variations

⑥ Use equipment to add variety to the stations. For example, have participants paddle across the pool while sitting on a kickboard, pick up objects from the bottom of the pool, or move across the pool keeping a ball between their legs.

⑥ Instead of setting up a circuit with specific activities in specific sections of the pool, have each person select the next activity by randomly picking a laminated activity card from a predetermined location (e.g., a floating cooler).

14.5   HYDRATED LAND SPORTS

8+

The Basics

The advantage of Hydrated Land Sports is that the majority of participants already know the basic rules. But the champions on land may find themselves surpassed in the water by the mermaids and mermen of the team. Play baseball in the water. Use a volleyball in place of a baseball and a kickboard in place of a bat. Everyone must stay in the pool at all times. Any ball hit out of the pool is considered a foul. Two fouls and the batter is out. People pitch to their own team. Otherwise, standard baseball rules apply.

How Many Participants?

Ten or more.

What Type of Equipment?

⑥ One volleyball.

⑥ One kickboard.

⑥ Four bases. Create bases by tying anything that floats to a heavy object.

Where?

Any swimming area.

Safety Considerations

⑥ Players can tag a runner (swimmer) with the ball only when they are holding it with two hands.

⑥ Be sure bases are at least 2 feet from the side of the pool.

Helpful Hints

⑥ If space is an issue, you can eliminate second base.

⑥ If the group has any nonswimmers, keep all of the bases in the shallow end.

Extensions and Variations

⑥ Water volleyball has the same rules as regular volleyball except that forearm passes are practically impossible. If the net cannot be at an adequate height, it may be necessary to outlaw spiking.

⑥ In water basketball, dribbling is not possible. Either allow people to move with the ball or force players to always pass. If backboards are not available, place trash cans on the pool deck.

⑥ Underwater hockey is a sport in and of itself, complete with world championships. However, its low profile (and virtually nonexistent spectator appeal) means that few people are familiar with it. Basically, the game uses an ice hockey puck that must remain on the bottom of the pool. Players have flippers, snorkels, and masks. In place of hockey sticks, players can use rubber spatulas (or specially made underwater hockey equipment). Because knuckles sometimes come out the worse for wear, gloves are recommended. This variation is intended for older, more experienced swimmers only.

About the Authors

Stephanie J. Hanrahan, PhD, is a senior lecturer in sport and exercise psychology at The University of Queensland in the department of human movement studies and the school of psychology, where she frequently interacts with coaches and athletes. Dr. Hanrahan is the 1997 recipient of The University of Queensland's Excellence in Teaching Award. She has made nearly 200 presentations about games to coaches and athletes, and she is the coauthor of *The Coaching Process: A Practical Guide to Improving Your Effectiveness.*

Dr. Hanrahan earned her doctorate in sport psychology from the University of Western Australia in 1989. She was a professional ice skater and an international-level volleyball player who received a sports scholarship in volleyball. She also has been a volleyball coach and a swimming and skating instructor.

Teresa D. Carlson, EdD, is a lecturer in physical education at The University of Queensland. She also taught high school physical education for 10 years in Botswana, Australia, Pakistan, and the United States.

Dr. Carlson has led more than 50 workshops for coaches and physical educators. She has written a book chapter and produced a video for teacher educators on adventure-based learning. She has been a competitive swimmer for more than 20 years and has coached netball, basketball, and track and field. Dr. Carlson earned her doctorate in teacher education from the University of Massachusetts in 1994.

Other Books From Human Kinetics

Teaching Sport Concepts and Skills
A Tactical Games Approach
Linda L. Griffin, PhD, Stephen A. Mitchell, PhD, and Judith L. Oslin, PhD
1997 • Paperback • 248 pp • ISBN 0-88011-478-9
$20.00 ($29.95 Canadian)

Changing Kids' Games
(Second Edition)
Don Morris and Jim Stiehl
1999 • Paperback • 160 pp • ISBN 0-88011-691-9
$17.00 ($25.50 Canadian)

Team Building Through Physical Challenges
Donald R. Glover, MS, and Daniel W. Midura, MEd
1992 • Paperback • 160 pp • ISBN 0-87322-359-4
$16.95 ($23.95 Canadian)

More Team Building Challenges
Daniel W. Midura, MEd, and Donald R. Glover, MS
1995 • Paperback • 120 pp • ISBN 0-87322-785-9
$14.95 ($20.95 Canadian)

The Competition-Cooperation Link
Games for Developing Respectful Competitors
Daniel W. Midura, MEd, and Donald R. Glover, MS
1999 • Paperback• 160 pp • ISBN 0-88011-850-4
$16.00 ($23.95 Canadian)

To request more information or to order, U.S. customers call
1-800-747-4457, e-mail us at **humank@hkusa.com,** or visit our Web site
at **www.humankinetics.com.** Persons outside the U.S. can contact us
via our Web site or use the appropriate telephone number, postal
address, or e-mail address shown in the front of this book.

 HUMAN KINETICS
The Information Leader in Physical Activity
P.O. Box 5076, Champaign, IL 61825-5076
2335